Advance Praise

"We all benefit when we create systems that work for everyone. Julie Kratz provides tools for individuals to drive systemic change as allies."

—Eve Rodsky
Author of *Fair Play* and *Find Your Unicorn Space*

"Not often do you find someone who can face their lived experience and empathize with other perspectives. Julie Kratz reveals her own truth eloquently so you can find yours too. Use this book to uncover the beauty in diversity and inclusion within your personal and professional life as well as take meaningful action."

—Ericka Young
Financial Coach
Author of *NAKED AND UNASHAMED 10 Money Conversations Every Couple Must Have*

"Allyship is a journey of choices, not a destination of character. By starting these conversations with our kids, and their communities of friends, we empower them to be change agents for equity organically and in real time. Educators and writers like Julie Kratz ensure that all of us have language and ideas at our disposal to do this important work."

—Daniel Juday
Inclusion Educator and Culture Coach

"If you're looking for the next step on your inclusion journey, here it is. The book provides concrete tools for allies to use at home and got me enthusiastic and motivated to make change!"

"What does it mean to be an ally? Julie Kratz explains the key attributes of allyship and how to do it at work and at home."

"All of our voices matter in DEI. Julie Kratz helps people understand how they can use their voices as allies effectively."

"To fully achieve equity in the workplace, we have to start at home. Julie Kratz explains key allyship actions and how to integrate these into our everyday lives at work and home."

"To lead like an ally requires you to step up and do hard work. Allyship in Action provides you with the tools you need for success. This book will enable you to be an invaluable diversity, equity, and inclusion partner. "

—Dr. Lynn Schmidt
Women's Rights Advocate and Speaker
Author of *Antisexist: Challenge Sexism, Champion Women's Rights, and Create Equality*

"Being an ally means taking action. Julie Kratz helps people understand how to take meaningful action to advance DEI individually and collectively."

—Nika White
President and CEO of Nika White Consulting

"When I think of an ally, I think of Julie Kratz and all the phenomenal work she's doing in this space to drive awareness. This book is yet another rexample of how much Julie deeply cares and is willing to get in the much to drive change forward. She gives personal reflections and strategies for moving the needle towards increased inclusion. Kudos to Julie on her latest masterpiece of bringing the collective together."

—Simone Morris
Inclusive Leadership and CEO
Simone Morris Enterprises

"Being an ally means doing something about DEI challenges. Julie Kratz helps people understand, and in particular White women understand, why their role is important to effecive DEI advocacy. She offers clear and practical steps anyone can take to address marginalization and exclusion, both individually with others that share your commitment to equity and inclusive values."

—Deborah Dagit
President, Deb Dagit Diversity LLC

"There is no on or off switch for diversity. It has to happen at home and at work for it to work. Julie Kratz articulates an amazing case for why well-meaning, good-hearted people need to shift from being passive to being ACTIVE in the curation of inclusion and belonging. Julie provides straightforward, actionable steps for everyone to practice being the change they wish to see in the world."

—**Angel G. Henry**
Author of *Dents in the Ceiling: Tools Women and Allies Need to Breakthrough*

"We all benefit when we create sustainable systems that advance intersectional justice. Julie Kratz provides specific examples and tools to help individuals advance justice and contribute to systemic change in their communities."

—**Lindsay Lyons, PhD**
Educational Justice Coach

ALLYSHIP IN ACTION

10 Practices for Living Inclusively

JULIE KRATZ

Next Pivot Point
by Julie Kratz

Next Pivot Point Publishing

Books may be ordered through booksellers or by contacting:
Julie Kratz

Next Pivot Point Publishing

julie@nextpivotpoint.com

NextPivotPoint.com

317-525-4310
13470 Shakamac Drive
Carmel, IN 46032

ISBN: 978-1-7365159-2-1 (paperback)
978-1-7365159-3-8 (eBook)

Table of Contents

Other Books by Julie Kratz

Allyship in Action Workbook: 10 Practices for Living Inclusively

Pivot Point: How to Build a Winning Career Game Plan

ONE: How Male Allies Support Women for Gender Equality

Lead Like an Ally: A Journey Through Corporate America with Strategies to Facilitate Inclusion

"Little Allies"

"Little Allies Coloring Book"

INTRODUCTION: MY ALLY JOURNEY

My daughter Jane started kindergarten in early August 2019. I remember our very first walk to the bus stop. It was a beautiful central Indiana morning, the sun shining down on our faces as we excitedly made our way. Jane beamed with joy as she gathered her things and got on the bus all by herself. I wept silently on the sidewalk as the bus pulled away, Jane still smiling from the window. It was bittersweet to see my little girl growing up.

In the following weeks I received several introductions and invitations to join the various parent organizations for Jane's school. One that stood out to me, given my line of work, was for a Parent Diversity, Equity, and Inclusion (DEI) Council. I was pleasantly surprised, considering Jane attends school in a predominantly White school district, and jumped at the opportunity to join other parents who shared my passion of teaching the next generation about the value of inclusion early in life.

We assembled in our community library for our first DEI Council meeting. Looking around at the other mothers, I noted that most of us were White. The topic of discussion was how to approach a conversation about diversity and inclusion with our young children. We believed that our children didn't yet understand complex things like racism, sexism, and homophobia. I wanted to protect my child, maybe even shelter her to some degree, but felt it was an important conversation to have. So how do I broach the subject? What do I do? It's a question a lot of White, straight, non-disabled parents struggle with.

As a White woman born and raised in the Midwest in the 1980s and 1990s, I was taught to be colorblind. Racism, sexism, and discrimination were of the past. My mother, well-intentioned, single, and White, told me that the world was equal for everyone now. The feminists, the Civil Rights Movement, and gay rights had all been addressed. In essence, if you work hard, you will be rewarded. That was the mantra repeated throughout my childhood.

So, imagine my surprise when I entered the workplace in the early 2000s and found out that was untrue. I was surrounded by an all-White, male leadership cohort with very few women, people of color, and other diverse representation to learn from.

As I was sitting in the DEI school council meeting, I realized that I didn't want my child to be raised with that same misconception. The myth of meritocracy (that hard work pays off) and encouraging our children to be colorblind (refusal to see color) does not teach our children about the world around them and the challenges that can hold people back.

You cannot solve a problem until you see it.

The Problems

What is the problem? There are differences everywhere. As humans, we naturally recognize these differences about one another and are curious about them. That is why children curiously point or ask questions about people with visible differences.

Problem #1: We All See Differences

According to Erin Winkler[1], "Research clearly shows that children not only recognize race from a very young age, but also develop racial biases by ages three to five."

Without education to understand these biases, they can be cemented by as early as age twelve. Children form biases about gender, race, sexual orientation, and abilities in their childhood years. Often, they come not directly from parents, but from the world around them (media, schools, friends, experiences, etc.).

---

[1] Winkler, "Children Are Not Colorblind."

FIGURE 2

Generation "Z-Plus" race-ethnic profile
(born since 2007)

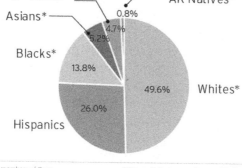

2+ Races *

Asians*

Blacks*

Hispanics

Am Indians/
AK Natives*

0.8%

4.7%

5.2%

13.8%

26.0%

49.6% Whites*

*Non Hispanic members of Race
Source: US Decennial Censuses and Census Population
Estimates, released June 21, 2018

B | Metropolitan Policy Program
at BROOKINGS

Problem #2: The Myth of Meritocracy

There is ample evidence that, despite our desire to believe in the myth of meritocracy, that idea is simply not true. Things are not getting better, either.

- Wealth gap[2] is ten times for White Americans than Black Americans
- Incarceration[3] for Black Americans is nearly five times the rate of White Americans
- Discipline rates[4] for Black children are two times higher than White kids for the same behavior

---

[2] McIntosh, Moss, and Shambaugh, "Examining the Black and White Wealth Gap."
[3] The Sentencing Project
[4] U.S. Department of Education, Office for Civil Rights, "School Climate and Safety."

- <u>Confidence</u>[5] drops for girls by thirty percent between the ages of eight and fourteen
- <u>Suicide rates</u>[6] for LGBTQ+ youth are four times higher than their peers
- <u>Disability</u>[7] affects three million children in the US, and is rising more rapidly for minority kids

As a White person who grew up in the lower middle class with low disposable income, I used to think that if I worked hard to get to where I am, why can't other people? Sure, I worked hard to get myself through college with good grades and earned a well-paying job. Why can't everyone else do the same thing? What I couldn't see, at the time, was that systems keep certain people down and other people up. As a female, I faced challenges, but I had it a lot easier than others because my skin color is white, I'm straight, cisgender (identifiying as the same gender of which you were assigned at birth), and non-disabled.

Problem #3: Lack of Education

Growing up, I didn't have resources to understand issues like race, gender, sexual orientation, disabilities, or any dimension of diversity. The notion of appreciating differences is well-intended, but not helpful when microaggressions (harmful statements about people who are different from us) are still commonplace. For example, my dad once told me that affirmative action was reverse racism, and on another occasion, my mom said it was okay to date a Black man, but not to marry a Black man.

---

[5] [Author] "Confidence Gap for Girls."
[6] The Trevor Project, "Estimate of How Often LGBTQ Youth Attempt Suicide in the U.S."
[7] Young and Crankshaw, "U.S. Childhood Disability Rate up in 2019 from 2008."

I can recall instances growing up when my Black friends would regularly get pulled over in our neighborhood. I didn't understand why because I did not get pulled over, not even one time, and so I said nothing. I deeply regret the time I told my light-skinned, Black friend, "You're like us, it's like you're White."

I had friends share with me (very bravely) that they were gay, and I questioned if they absolutely knew for sure. I am truly embarrassed that I was complicit with racism, sexism, and homophobia growing up and, without knowing better, committing microaggressions that harmed my friends. My parents certainly didn't know how to teach me to be better because they didn't know any better. In hindsight, there were so many opportunities to use my voice, but I did not know that I needed to, nor did I know how.

DEI is personal.

The Journey to Solutions

In my experience, going to college was the first time I was in a truly diverse environment. At Ohio State University, I relished in an environment with lots of different ethnicities, gender identities, races, and folks with various lived experiences. I soaked up every experience I could find on campus. My friends would joke that I would find the person most different from myself at a social event and find a way to have a heart-to-heart with them.

It was there, at Ohio State, that I discovered my love for diversity, but then I didn't know it was something you could do for a living. So instead, I studied Business and Women's Studies. Women's Studies opened my eyes to gender bias, but I realize now it was flawed. It centered on White women's experiences, and thus reinforced the divide-and-conquer strategy between women and people of color.

I went on to spend twelve years in Corporate America before starting my own DEI training business in 2015. I rarely saw myself reflected in leadership roles, and never felt a sense of psychological safety and belonging in the White, male-dominated space. I now speak with organizations and leaders on how to be allies for diversity and inclusion. Yet having the same conversations at home is nuanced and challenging. Since starting my business, I have poured my heart and soul and countless hours into learning and understanding all that I can about inclusion.

An ally is someone who supports others who are different from themself. That could be by race, gender, ethnicity, sexual orientation, abilities, or other dimensions of difference. An ally could be a friend, a mentor, a caregiver, a family member, or someone in your life personally and/or professionally. There is no one-size-fits-all definition, and allyship cannot be self-proclaimed. It is often defined in the eye of the beholder.

DEI is about progress over perfection.

I, by no means, have all the answers. DEI is a journey, not a destination. We're all allies-in-training. I still fumble as an ally. Over the years I have read dozens of books on anti-racism and inclusion, and I always ignorantly believe I have the answers when I begin a new book. I think to myself, *I already know how to solve this problem.* And I'm wrong, every single time. I always have more to learn. Embracing the growth mindset can help us see past what we think we know already. I remind myself of one of my favorite leadership quotes, "You don't know what you don't know."

While on the topic of what I do not know, I am White. That means I will never fully understand the lived experiences of people of color. I am straight and cisgender, and I will never fully understand the experiences of the LGBTQ+ community. I am non-disabled (at the time of writing this book) and do not fully understand the experiences of people with disabilities. I acknowledge that because I am associated with the majority group in many areas (White, straight, cisgender, non-disabled), I have access to privilege. For instance:

- I don't worry about being targeted by or mistreated by police.
- If I were to go missing, the mainstream news headlines would more than likely feature my story.
- People see me as someone who looks trusting and approachable.
- I am not asked where I am from (or where am I *really* from) often.
- I read books with people like me centered as main characters.
- I don't worry about having accommodations to do my work properly.
- My hair is easy to buy products for.
- I feel safe being open about my partner at work.
- People don't refer to my friends and family as "you ___ people."
- I can wear a hoodie and not be seen as suspicious.
- I don't worry about being incarcerated.
- Decision-makers will listen to me.
- It is a choice to share my pronouns.
- People look like me at my local library, grocery, school, bank, etc.
- I can speak out openly about diversity and feel psychologically safe doing so.

- I don't have to prepare my children for the world to treat them differently based on their skin color.

Looking back, the summer of 2020 was turbulent to say the least, but it brought about change. My then six-year-old daughter would ask tough questions like, "Why do Black people have to die, Mommy?" as we watched the coverage of the murders of George Floyd, Ahmaud Arbery, and Breonna Taylor. I had no answer for that one, except tears.

That same summer we purchased the new Crayola crayons that feature different skin tones (released for the first time), and she drew a picture of her asking a child of color to be her friend. I cried again (White guilt is real). She sees color and she sees difference as additive. She is naturally curious about differences, and she wants to know more about them.

Now Jane is eight, and as a White girl, she has observed racism in her day-to-day interactions at school. She shared with me an instance when she was riding home on her school bus with a classmate (who happened to be a child of color) and another kid said, "You cannot marry him, it's illegal." On another occasion, she felt confusion when another friend of color was bullied and then labeled as "emotional" for defending themself.

Well-intentioned parents might say it's too early to teach them these things. I disagree. Most children experience or observe discrimination. My dear friend and co-host of our *Inclusion School Podcast*, Simone Morris, shared a story with me when we first met. Her daughter, Millie, was only three years old when she was told that she did not belong while playing on the playground at pre-school. The conversation sparked *Inclusion School Podcast*, which exists to help caregivers, educators, and parents by providing insight, information, and context so that they can have brave conversations about diversity and inclusion. We still don't have all the answers, but we remain curious to learn more.

As an adult, I have witnessed the same behaviors, but now I choose to call people out and challenge their harmful beliefs and statements. Needless to say, it has led to several very uncomfortable conversations and disagreements. I am swimming against the current myself, unlearning history, and relearning it through a DEI lens will be a lifetime effort. When I started doing DEI work seven years ago, I honestly didn't know what I was getting myself into. I had no idea how deep-rooted and systemic these problems are. I was naive and uneducated. I wanted the world to be better and so I just kept showing up.

I'm thankful that I have the opportunity to be a part of this conversation each day because I truly believe it makes us all better humans. It's helped me become a better partner, caregiver, parent, friend, and family member. As I've learned to better appreciate that all humans have different lived experiences, it has broadened my thinking, ability to empathize, and growth.

There is not (and never was) an on or off switch for DEI at home and/or at work.

My experience as a DEI practitioner motivated me to lean into the conversation at home as well. I am sure that anyone who is passionate about DEI understands that change doesn't stop at work. The 2020s taught us that change is inevitable. Corporate America has become more global, hybrid work is commonplace, and power has shifted to employees over employers.

According to Pew Research Center,[8] seventy-five percent of people expect their employers to drive inclusion, and they also look to their co-workers and leaders to speak up about hard things. Gone are the days of leaving your personal life at home, clocking into a workplace, and being a different version of you. As global citizens, we need to model the behavior for others to follow. In the book *The Good Guys*, co-authors Brad Johnson and David Smith help White men understand how to be better allies. They shared the concept of "global citizenship" in their recent *Harvard Business Review* article.

Global citizenship[9] "is the idea that people have rights and responsibilities that come with being a citizen of the entire world, rather than a particular nation or place."

Some of the competencies included are self-awareness, respect for difference, curiosity, flexibility, empathy, and intercultural knowledge. These competencies are also commonly used in corporate settings to evaluate performance. According to HBR,[10] research reveals those leaders who truly believe in the value proposition of diversity, inclusion, and the core tenets of allyship are sixty-two percent more likely to occupy the C-suite. Inclusive leadership will be more valued in the future.

We must start the DEI conversation earlier.

Teaching kids and family about inclusion helps them learn to be inclusive leaders and to navigate future workplaces that will be incredibly diverse and competing on a global scale—essentially, teaching them how to be leaders who

---

[8] Menasce Horowitz, "Americans See Advantages and Challenges in Growing Racial and Ethnic Diversity."

[9] Participate Learning, "Global Competencies."

[10] Smith, Johnson, and Stromberg, "How Men Can Be More Inclusive Leaders."

will be effective in the world they will be living in. Holding onto the status quo is not helpful. Pivoting to more inclusive behaviors will help our children, friends, and families be more relevant and create more opportunity for them in their future.

White women have a role to play in DEI.

Overwhelmingly, women of color are the majority of DEI practitioners. We need more White, straight, cisgender, non-disabled people involved in this conversation. White women are in a unique position to be allies for change. Torn between the systems of patriarchy that we do not benefit from, and the systems of white supremacy that we do benefit from, White women have been taught to hold back.

We have our own gendered experience to empathize from, yet that is far from understanding deep-rooted racism, ableism, and homophobia. By our proximity to the hierarchy of White men, we have a great deal of influence, where the lion's share of wealth and decision-making lies. We also have proximity to the next generation of little allies as educators.

Eighty percent of K-12 educators are White and seventy-seven percent are women. NEA News.[11]

Karen Fleshman, DEI speaker and ally, explained the importance of White women in the DEI conversation best: As number two on the social hierarchy, White women dance between power and marginalization. They are well-positioned to influence systems for positive change.

---

[11] Walker, "Who Is the Average U.S. Teacher?"

DEI is not a zero-sum game.

White women, along with our allies, can fight the old school priming of the divide-and-conquer strategy, the message that we cannot fight multiple systems of oppression at once, most commonly, race and gender. Rather than fight these battles independently, what if we collectively addressed all human issues together? Rather than look at this as a finite my-pie-slice-vs.-your-pie-slice game, what if the pie gets bigger when we work together? What if we are all stronger when we work together?

While White women certainly have a unique position to speak up about diversity, they are often seen as not having *skin in the game*. It is always better to partner with people already existing in this space. Before writing this book, I scoured through resources to help me navigate this conversation.

DEI is a paradox.

Simone and I had the same intention when creating the *Inclusion School Podcast* several years ago. It is meant to add to the conversation. To be clear, this is a "both and" conversation because there is rarely a right or wrong answer. DEI is a paradox. We need to hold two different points of view simultaneously to be inclusive.

Chainsawsuit.com

DEI might seem controversial to those who do not understand. In my local school district (and I'm sure in many across the US), there has been controversy over focusing on DEI. Some parents feel strongly that DEI should not be taught in the classroom and should only be within parents' control. What they don't realize is that these are basic principles to help kids be better humans and understand the complexities of life that they will certainly face (like my young children are already facing), and they need language and tools to process these experiences.

Silence is compliance.

The Barriers

As humans, we fear what we don't understand. This fear can feel very real for people. There are three main categories of fear leading parents, caregivers, and educators to withdraw from the DEI conversation.

- **The Expert Effect:** In DEI, we rarely have all the answers. More often, we have questions and have to listen to others explain the issues they're experiencing to fully understand them. That's really uncomfortable when we've also been taught that we need to have the answers. One of the hardest things to say to a child or friend is "I don't know" and still seem credible.
- **Protector Mode.** Well-intentioned people avoid hard conversations like DEI because they can conjure up feelings of guilt and shame. Teaching DEI does not shame people; it frees them to learn about differences, and learning requires discomfort.
- **In Control.** We love to be in control. Letting go of the control and being open to new ways of thinking becomes harder as our brains mature. Uncovering and confronting our own biases requires us to release control and co-create a better future for all, together.

As allies, it is important to carry others' stories with us. When someone shares their stories with you, it's important to believe them and not to shame them or ask, "What were you doing to cause this?" or question their perceptions of what happened. True allies listen without judgment. If you happen to hear a story more than once, or stories feel eerily familiar, there's a high likelihood that this is a universal experience that people within that dimension of diversity have in common.

White privilege just means not having to think about your skin color.

All of my friends of color who have children have shared heartbreaking stories with me about their children being told by other kids that they couldn't be played with or they didn't belong based on their skin color. They were told these messages from a very young age. No child should ever feel less than based on something like their skin color, which they have no control over.

In addition, my friends of color who are parents have shared that they, as a necessary precaution, will have the "talk" with their children about when (not if) they are pulled over by the police and how to handle the potentially dangerous situation (where to put your hands, keep your ID, etc.).

Because of my own learning journey and difficulty talking about tough issues like racism, sexism, and homophobia in my personal life, I decided to write this book. When I compared notes with other White parents, DEI practitioners, my gay friends, my friends of color, and my own family, I realized no one knew how to fully navigate DEI in their personal lives and with their own children. I wanted to put together a set of tools to help.

This is by no means the answer to extremely complex problems. These are ideas and tools that I've uncovered and learned and now rely on to help me with my own journey from work to home.

Allyship is a Choose Your Own Adventure.

As you continue reading, consider your allyship path to be non-linear. Dig into skills that matter most to you. Each chapter focuses on one skill of allyship at home with a set of tools, additional resources to learn more, and an assessment to evaluate where you are on your ally journey so that you can continue to measure your progress over time. While this is not a fully exhaustive list,

I have found these tenets to be most helpful when having conversations with children, friends, and family outside of work.

- **Why.** Without a strong emotional reason to do this work, it's really easy to fall into the performative ally trap where participation fluctuates with the news cycle. Allies consistently use their voices for positive change.
- **Empathy.** The quintessential allyship skill. Allyship requires us to let go of control and is not about us being the expert or the protector. We have to listen to learn as allies.
- **Vulnerability**. It's accepting that we do not have all of the answers that separates us as allies.
- **Curiosity.** As children, we are naturally curious, and we unlearn how to be curious as we grow older. In taking a lead from younger people, we can really learn this important ally trait.
- **Emotions.** Being mindful and separating facts from emotions that are part of difficult conversations can be tricky as an ally. Allies meet people where they're at and they help to create psychologically safe places.
- **Courage.** If this were easy, we wouldn't be having this same tired conversation about DEI. You're not alone. The first step is deciding to do something.
- **Coaching.** Conversations with DEI will get candid. Practicing a coaching mindset instead of a teaching mindset can help expand conversations where both parties learn and grow.
- **Accountability.** Personal as well as shared accountability for our actions collectively matters. This means modeling the behaviors that we want to see from others as we're learning and growing so that others will be motivated to join us as allies.

- **Privilege.** Acknowledging the benefits we have by association with the majority group is important to understand. Allies leverage their privilege to uplift others.
- **Inspiration**. Part of allyship is calling others into the DEI conversation, especially those with privilege and power.

As you begin your journey, be sure to protect your energy, practice good self-care, and know this work is important, worthwhile, and will have an impact. This work has ups and downs. It will not be a straight path and can be very humbling. To stay on course, it is important to visualize success.

Begin your ally journey by reflecting on...

- What the future could look like with more allies?
- How DEI conversations could spur positive change for others?
- How you could be a part of the change you want to see in the world?

For me, it's seeing a world that is more inclusive for my daughters, for my friends of color, for my gay friends, for my friends with disabilities, and for fellow DEI practitioners that are tired of having this same conversation over and over. We can and will do better—together.

If we are waiting for perfect allies, we will wait forever.

Hold that visual in your mind. Keep that positive focus as you navigate the murky waters of allyship. Allies do hard things. They stay active in the face of adversity. If you want to lead like an ally in your personal life as well as work life, all aboard. We are stronger together as allies.

CHAPTER ONE: WHY

We all are a product of our lived experiences. This means that everything we experience from early childhood to adulthood shapes the way we behave, our expectations, and how we learn to communicate with the world around us. The earliest guidance given to us is from our caregivers. For some, that's your biological parents; for others, that could be grandparents, foster parents, adopted parents, aunts and uncles, and other friends or family members.

As humans, we are wired to recognize patterns. We have done that since our earliest days to survive. When our brains are presented with a new situation that we haven't yet experienced or someone hasn't modeled for us, we are often paralyzed. For instance, as a child, I was told very often to "figure it out." I had a single mother growing up who did not have the time or resources to deal with my inquisitive nature. I didn't know how to figure it out a lot of the time and so I struggled because I was afraid I would make a mistake. While my mother did the best she could, that lack of guidance for decision-making left me with a lot of discomfort to make decisions as a young person, but ultimately led me to cultivate the ability to easily make decisions with ambiguity in adulthood.

There's no wrong or right here. The point is that we're accumulating these experiences and lessons from a very young age. That repeated phrase that I was told growing up, "figure it out," reinforced the myth of meritocracy for me into my early adulthood. I believed that because I had to figure it out as a kid, certainly others could figure their own way out of their challenges. This might be true for innocent everyday decisions, as I did with homework and friend conflicts, but it's certainly not true for complex situations involving race, gender, sexual orientation, and abilities.

It is clear to me that I still hold onto this bias today. Now, as a parent, I find myself echoing that same statement to my children. I'm confronted with the challenges of repeating past mistakes and realize that the only way to depart from destructive patterns is to recognize them in my actions and words and make the conscious decision to change my behaviors.

Identify the Patterns

Our brains are constantly observing and recording our experiences for our own survival. If there's a new experience, especially one that's scary, our brain is likely to record it and recall it at a much higher rate than a positive experience. For many folks, difficult conversations about things you don't fully understand can evoke fear. We call this the expert effect. We feel a lot more comfortable talking about subjects we understand than we do the more complex and ambiguous topics.

"Deep down, at our cores, there are only two emotions: love and fear." Elisabeth Kübler-Ross

Fear, if left unaddressed, can cause us to withdraw from conversations about DEI. Our fear of the unknown, and situations we haven't experienced, is what challenges what we know to be true and causes our brains to send off alarm bells. Our brain often misperceives new concepts as threats, triggering the fight-or-flight response from our brain's amygdala. As DEI is new information for the brain to process for most in the majority group (White, male, cisgender, straight, non-disabled), even the well-intentioned might take issue or avoid conversations about DEI altogether because of this fear.

DEI is change, and change can be hard for people. I'd like you to be honest with yourself. How open are you to change? Do you embrace it, or avoid it at all cost? There's no right or wrong answer. It's about understanding yourself and your relationship with new concepts, information, and change. It's acknowledging that some folks might need time to process, some may be ready instantly, and others may be sitting on the fence because they're afraid to say or do the wrong thing.

According to the RightTrack Learning poll[12], when it comes to talking about diversity and inclusion at work, fifty-five percent of people are scared to say the wrong thing. I believe the same rings true at home. Our discomfort with potentially disrupting the relationships that matter the most to us can be stressful. When someone brings up diversity in a social setting, I've seen the room go silent. I've watched people struggle to make eye contact and find excuses to leave the conversation. We have to make room for DEI, and that begins with talking about it.

We fear what we don't understand.

To become an ally at home, you have to be willing to recognize certain patterns and interrupt them. Some reflections to better understand your patterns:

- How comfortable do you feel with ambiguity and change?

---

[12] Right Track Learning poll, Twitter.

- What messages do you remember hearing or witnessing about race, gender, sexual orientation, and disabilities growing up?
- Think about your relationships growing up with people different from yourself. What were your perceptions of your friends, family members, and others who were different from you?

These questions will help you uncover your comfort level with DEI and any patterns that may need to be disrupted for yourself and others. It's never too late to broaden your outlook, and although our hardwiring gets more entrenched as we age, it is always malleable. The key is to identify the patterns so they can be corrected.

Fear-based patterns only work when we let them go unnoticed. One way to correct them is to name them. Close your eyes and think about your greatest fears. Now, take a deep breath, exhale, and write them down. Do any of these look familiar to you? Public speaking, abandonment, losing a loved one, being fired, not being loved, relationships ending, not getting a promotion, losing something you want or need?

Now try the same exercise with DEI. What are your greatest fears related to becoming an ally and discussing DEI? Be honest, what scares you the most? Close your eyes, embrace the fears for a couple minutes, and then write them all down unfiltered. Do any of these come to mind? Being irrelevant, making someone mad, looking silly, missing out on an opportunity for yourself, people not accepting your message, being misunderstood, being judged by someone you care about?

Select your top three and label them. For example, if you fear being judged unfairly, which then causes you to avoid speaking up to people whom you perceive as behaving non-inclusively, you might label your fear "avoidance."

We take the power away from fear when we label it. When we give it a name, it can no longer feel so scary. When a fear is unaddressed or uncertain, our brain does not know how to process it and often fills in that uncertainty with the worst-case scenario.

If you were to talk openly about the DEI in your personal life, what is the worst thing that could happen?

My guess is that the worst-case scenario that you imagined isn't likely to happen, and hopefully, it isn't as bad as the fear you were feeling before you recognized it.

A few years ago, when my daughter was in kindergarten, I sat down with her to discuss Martin Luther King Jr. Day. In preparation, we had previously borrowed a few books from the library to educate ourselves and help stimulate a conversation. After reading the books, she had some really honest questions. She wanted to know more about what happened to Martin Luther King Jr. I answered he was shot and killed. She asked why he was killed. I replied, at that time, some White people were afraid of his message. She then asked why White people were scared. At that point, I started crying and thought to myself, *Where do I begin? This must be why White people don't talk about this!*

I share this because this was one of my "worst-case scenarios." Not having the right words to say, not helping her learn and understand such a historically important message. I was paralyzed with fear because I wanted to be the expert. I was not in control, and I desperately did not want her to feel shame because she is White.

For me and Jane, it has been an uphill journey since we began our conversations on Martin Luther King Jr. Day.

We are heading in the right direction, having found better content, videos, stories, and experiences to have more open conversations about Martin Luther King Jr. Even though our start was difficult, it was a necessary experience for both me and Jane to learn and grow.

Meet our children where they are at.

We learn from our mistakes, and I believe that I had to make that mistake and feel that pain to be able to have more candid conversations with Jane and others in the future. If I had not leaned into that conversation, I wouldn't have had the confidence to discuss more complex topics with Jane, like the long overdue social justice movement of 2020, Black Lives Matter, and racism.

Rewrite the Scripts

Many adults say that children are innocent and that we shouldn't teach them about the harsh realities of the world too soon. The belief that we should protect or shield them is known as protector mode. While children are innocent, they are also experiencing the world around them every second of every day. From the television shows they watch, the children they play with, and the conversations they hear around them, their brains are taking it all in. They are not as sheltered as we like to think they are, unfortunately.

Now that you have been able to identify some of your fears, worst-case scenarios, and your own challenges navigating DEI conversations at home, ask yourself the following to gain more clarity:

- How do I know that is true?
- What information do I have to support that fear?
- What is possible?
- What if nothing changes? How will I feel?

The first two questions challenge the assumption you have that your fear is legitimate. The second two questions help you shift from a fear-based, fixed mindset to an abundance, growth mindset. For you to be able to understand and correct these fears, your brain has to visualize a future that's positive, a future that you want. If you have your own limitations because of your lack of exposure to diverse lived experiences, it's time to shift the fear of what you don't know to what you could know. So, get curious and be open to learning new things. That subtle shift in language is powerful. Our brains believe what we feed it.

While I was writing this book, I posted a picture of the book *Raising White Kids* by Jennifer Harvey on LinkedIn. I found the book to be really helpful in the research for improving allyship at home and a great resource for race-conscious parenting. I shared a picture of the book cover with the caption, "As a White woman raising White girls, it's important to have proactive conversations about race so they can learn to be better allies." In the days following, there were a plethora of comments, both encouraging and discouraging. While some (White) parents were upset with the content (I imagine, without reading more about the book), many people of color offered words of encouragement. My feed was filled with polarizing comments, and I was uncomfortable.

I thought to myself, *What have I done? Did I do something wrong? Should I rewrite my post or take it down altogether?* Thankfully, I didn't do either. I sifted through the comments and reported those that were harmful or threatening but left the comments that had opposing viewpoints. In this social conversation, it's not about being right or wrong; it's about being willing to listen to learn.

Let the fear go.

By leaving the (appropriate) opposing comments on my post, a wonderful thing happened. One commenter garnered several replies. He originally shared that he was opposed to the idea of teaching DEI to children, but after reading the many replies to his post, he stated that he was willing to learn more. That's what happens when we let go of our fears and embrace change. We become more open and inclusive. It took several patient people on that thread to help him find his way into the conversation. As a result, he may be able to convince others like him to embrace change some day. That is what is possible when you let go of fear.

Start with You

You can want others to change, but you only have the power to change yourself. Just like what happened with my LinkedIn post, ultimately the only person who could change that person's viewpoint was them. I find this paradigm shift to be true in my DEI work with clients as well.

While facilitating a corporate DEI training kickoff for a new client recently, I received a private message from someone. They had taken issue with my use of the word "privilege" and felt it was offensive. They then went on to explain how their life had been difficult and that they had worked hard to get to where they were in life. My understanding was that they felt like my use of the word "privilege" had undermined their lived experiences and work ethic.

At that moment, I was in the middle of training and did not have the time to properly address them. I later shared the feedback with the client and offered some strategies to approach the individual one-on-one. I checked back in a week later and reported that they had a very positive conversation. My client explained that it had been this person's first experience with DEI training and they just didn't know what to expect. They are now open to learning new things, but my use of the word "privilege" early on in the training had jarred them.

I see misunderstandings like this every day. I could have easily written off that person as incapable of change, even racist or sexist, if I let my mind go down that fear path. I could have made a lot of assumptions without even knowing this person beyond that one comment. I knew for my client to be successful, there had to be a common ground. I didn't want someone to not participate in DEI conversations because they simply just didn't understand a phrase (note: more on privilege in Chapter Nine).

DEI work at home can be taxing because sometimes it feels as though you are carrying the weight of other people's problems. Creating space to listen when you desperately want your own voice to be heard, looking in the mirror instead of pointing a finger the other way, is not easy. If it were easy to do these things, we wouldn't need books on the subject.

"Be the change that you wish to see in the world." Mahatma Gandhi

The key is to set aside differences and look instead for commonalities. If you want others to listen, be sure to listen first. If you want others to be more open-minded, be more open-minded yourself. If you want others to embrace DEI, model it positively for them to see and, hopefully, embrace as well.

Reflect on this: What is my role in creating positive change?

What kind of ally do you want to be? An ally is someone who is helpful to someone different from themself. That may be a neighbor, children, friends, or family. While this book is a guide for personal relationships, of course, you can have allies at work too.

Do you want to be a better friend, a more inclusive parent or caregiver, or help your family become more open-minded? Being inclusive at home starts with your behavior, modeling yourself what you want to see from others. As humans, we have mirror neurons in our brains. What that means is that we subconsciously observe the behavior of others and then mirror it to fit in. That is why babies instinctively smile when we smile at them. This is also why we start adopting habits of other people who we spend time with. This is an innate human response. If you want to change the behaviors or beliefs of others you care about, it really does start with doing what you want others to do more of.

Kids mirror what they see in the world.

Remember, allyship is a journey, not a destination. There are no shortcuts and no instant wins. It can feel like one step forward and then two steps back at times. Please don't let that discourage you. Our behaviors are based on the culmination of our life experiences. Unlearning what we believe to be true, shifting our perspectives, and being open to learning new things takes time, and our brains don't like to change. We are fighting our primitive hardwiring, so to speak.

Allies do hard things. They lean into positive change and model it for others. Before moving ahead to the next chapter, take some time to assess yourself and craft your ally why and vision.

Ally Why Exercise: A strong why tells the world why DEI is important to you personally. It could be about your friends or family, your upbringing, or your own genuine wish for the world to be more inclusive. It should be specific to you and short enough that you can remember it to share with others. For me, my ally why is: I want the future to be more inclusive for the next generation of little allies. Your ally why could start with a strong "I" statement with action verbs like aspire, commit, want, strive, etc. We cannot self-proclaim to be allies, so avoid words like "am."

Ally Vision Exercise: The key here is focus. What kind of ally do you want to be? How do you want to show up for others who are different from you? That could be a mentor, a friend, a confidant, a trusted advisor, a challenger, and/or an advocate. Allyship takes on lots of different forms. Remember, this is a Choose Your Own Adventure. Concise, easy-to-share statements work best. For me, my ally vision is: I help facilitate inclusive spaces where all people feel seen, heard, and like they belong. Your ally vision could paint an aspirational picture that is currently not happening today and with your allyship will be possible in the future.

You will find at the end of each chapter a short assessment to help you evaluate where you currently are and where you want to be as an ally. Consider the assessment results today your starting point on your ally journey. Think about what success looks like for you with your ally vision and why. Focus on a few statements that, with practice, you could get better. Always remember, it's not about being a perfect ally; it's about making positive progress.

Assessment:

- ☐ I feel comfortable with ambiguity and change.
- ☐ I have identified the problematic messaging that I may have received about race, gender, sexual orientation, and disabilities growing up.
- ☐ I look for opportunities to disrupt and correct my own unhelpful patterns that are non-inclusive.
- ☐ I realize my own limitations based on my lived experiences (or lack of lived experiences).
- ☐ I believe that change starts with me.
- ☐ I model inclusive behavior for others.
- ☐ I look at non-inclusive conflicts as opportunities to learn and grow.
- ☐ I believe people are capable of positive change.
- ☐ I have a strong ally why.
- ☐ I have an ally vision that will keep me focused even when it is hard.

Daily habits are critical for allyship at home. Journaling can be a helpful tool to record any positive behavior change you're hoping to make in your life. With intentional, consistent focus, you will see results at much higher rates. Consider some daily journal prompts to help align your ally why:

- ☐ How did I use my voice?
- ☐ What fears did I face or uncover?
- ☐ What conversations did I have that were helpful?

- ☐ What am I thankful for someone sharing with me?
- ☐ What new information have I learned?
- ☐ Which of my perspectives or beliefs are changing?
- ☐ How am I connecting with my ally why?
- ☐ What steps have I taken to be closer to my ally vision?
- ☐ What is one way I hope to grow more?
- ☐ How can I share my journey with others?

Why Reader Activity 1
Childhood Reflections

Discuss your answers to these questions with a person or two whom you trust:

1. Growing up, what kind of messages did you hear about race/gender/disabilities/LGBTQ+ (colorblindness, boys/girls do this, etc.)?

2. What problematic statements do you remember yourself or others saying (retarded, gay as pejorative, etc.)?

3. What exposure did you have to other races, ethnicities, LGBTQ+, people with disabilities, etc.?

Guides at the end of each chapter created with the help of Instructional Designer, Elizabeth Davis

Why Reader Activity 2
Dimensions of Diversity Inventory

What dimensions of diversity do you identify with? Circle or check all that apply to you.

Wealth
- -Rich
- -Middle Class
- -Poor

Body Size
- -Slim
- -Average
- -Large

Language
- -English-speaking
- -Learned English
- -Non-English/Monolingual

Housing
- -Owns Property
- -Rents Property
- -Homeless

Mental Health
- -Robust Mental Health
- -Mostly Stable Mental Health
- -Vulnerable Mental Health

Formal Education
- -Post-Secondary
- -High School
- -Elementary School

Gender
- -Cisgender Man
- -Cisgender Woman
- -Trans/Intersex/Nonbinary

Sexuality
    -Heterosexual
    -Gay, Lesbian, Bi, Pan, Asexual

Citizenship
    -US Citizen
    -Documented US Citizen
    -Undocumented US Citizen

Neurodiversity
    -Neurotypical
    -Some Neurodivergence
    -Significant Neurodivergence

Skin Color
    -White
    -Black
    -Brown

Ability
    -Non-disabled
    -Mildly Disabled
    -Severely Disabled

Have a conversation with someone you know personally and with whom you have high trust. Compare dimensions and discuss these questions:

1. What identities are most important to you?
2. What identities have you felt like you needed to cover or hide?
3. What shifted for you when looking at your dimensions?
4. What did you learn?

Why Group or Family Activity

After you have taken your own inventory on your dimensions of diversity and discussed with someone, do this activity with your group or family so that they can start to take their own inventory of their dimensions of diversity.

Materials:
- 1-2 pieces of blank white paper per child
- Coloring utensils (try to make sure there are different colors for skin color—do a Google search for 'multiracial coloring utensils' you can purchase online, or look for these in stores)
- A drawing you (the parent/caretaker) created of yourself with your family at your home (doesn't need to be anything amazing)

Directions:
1. Show the group what you drew and explain each part of what you drew so that they can hear your dimensions of diversity clearly. Then, put your drawing away so that kids don't feel like they need to copy off of yours for the activity.
2. Tell the group it's their turn to draw their family the way they want to. Allow them time to draw.
3. Come back together as a group and discuss these questions:
   a. What do you see that is similar in your drawings?
   b. What do you see that is different in your drawings?
   c. Share your favorite thing about yourself.
   d. Share your favorite thing about your home.

e. Share something you drew differently than what is true in real life (refer back to something you may have drawn differently because it's a dimension you've learned to hide or change).
f. What did you learn from this activity?

Say:
"This is just our group/family, but think about how many other families and people are different than we are. We all have different stories and experiences. Some of us may look similar on the outside, but when we get to know each other, we realize that we all have very different life stories. Isn't it cool how we are all so different? It means that we can learn so much from each other. Imagine how cool it is when we work together, bring our stories, and share our strengths for the common good of others. But think about how much pain, hurt, and brokenness comes when we speak words of hate, when we judge others before getting to know them, when we won't become friends with others, or when we are completely alone. A lot of the world is experiencing those things. How does that make you feel to know that? That's why I'm so glad we are learning together. We want to become allies. An ally is someone who stands up for others and is a friend to others—even if no one else around them is. It's hard work to become an ally because the rest of the world is often doing the opposite. We want to become allies to the people who are often pushed to the side, forgotten, lonely, hurt, judged, and mistreated. We'll spend the next few weeks learning how to do that, but honestly, it's a lifelong process to learn how to show up for others."

CHAPTER TWO: EMPATHY

Our idea of empathy stems from what we were taught growing up. I'm sure at some point you heard either one or both of these phrases: "Put yourself in someone else's shoes," and "What if that were you? How would you feel?" The problem is that both of those statements miss the mark of true empathy because it is more than just pretending to be someone else. In fact, it's impossible to be somebody else or wear their shoes. I wear a size nine and a half wide women's shoe. I know for a fact how hard it is to find someone with my exact same shoe size.

No one knows what it is like to wear your shoes.

Children understand the difficulty of empathy. When challenged to pretend to be someone else, they often respond with, "I'm not someone else, I am me." We see the world through our own eyes, through our own lived experiences. It's impossible to only see the world through someone else's eyes because you can't possibly have the full context of all of their cumulative lived experiences.

I have white skin, I identify as straight, I am cisgender, and I am non-disabled. I can never fully understand what it is like to be a person of color, a member of the LGBTQ+ community, or someone with a disability, but that doesn't mean that I get a free pass to check out. Instead, it means that I have the opportunity to be allies to others with different lived experiences from my own.

As a woman, I believe that I can empathize with the experiences of those who are different from me who are underrepresented. I can relate to what it is like to be the only person in the room who looks like me. I can understand how it feels to be interrupted or have ideas that aren't taken seriously or acknowledged. I have had similar experiences. While my experiences might be similar, and can be sources of common ground, my experiences are unique to me. It is important to remember that as an ally I cannot project those experiences onto someone else. I cannot assume that all people of color have the same experiences or, just because someone identifies as a woman, they too share the same experiences as me.

Empathy is more of a bridge to understanding someone else's world. Pretending like you know what it's like to be someone else is unfair. Allyship centers around empathy. Always seek out common ground with others, especially when it feels like there is none. It is impossible to feel love and hate at the same time. Looking for things about someone you love rather than detest opens up the doors to empathy.

Perspective-Taking

Rather than pretending to be someone else, try instead to find out what perspective they might have, and is most important when it is different from your perspective.

Perspective-taking is defined as trying on the perspective of another without fully agreeing or understanding the complexity of their perspective. Then, you can search to uncover and learn why they may have that perspective.

Remember the five whys framework (who, what, when, where, why, and how)? Chances are you learned this as a child. You can use this problem-solving framework to investigate. Problems can be complex and multi-layered, and solving one part of a problem rarely addresses the full problem. I compare it to looking at the tip of an iceberg. You cannot see what is below the surface of the water. By asking the five whys, you can go "under the surface" of the problem so that you can have a clearer understanding and take measures to solve it.

Once they learn how to speak, toddlers can be very inquisitive. If you've been around small children, you know they ask a lot of questions. They seek to understand why things are the way they are and all too frequently ask the question "why?" about *everything*.

Why do we lose this curious nature as we get older? It's because our brains are able to recognize patterns, make assumptions based on those patterns, and stop thinking of other possibilities. This is based on the understanding that extra thinking requires mental energy that could be saved for harder tasks. The brain is an energy-conserving organ. This simple thinking might be helpful for remembering how a stapler works, turning on your computer, or other mundane tasks, but it is not so helpful when interacting with others.

People are complex and rarely fit into nice, clean boxes. In relation to diversity and differences, our brains will oversimplify and categorize by race and gender because we think we can see these categories (and oftentimes cannot). We need to help our minds broaden the definition of diversity beyond just race and gender to understand the array of uniqueness that makes us human beings.

DEI is more than race and gender.

In my corporate DEI training work, I often display a piece of ambiguous artwork that can be interpreted as many different images. Some say it looks like a face, a coat, and others see a dark hallway. I've had so many interesting responses when presenting this artwork. The point of the exercise isn't to get it right, but to share what you see and then compare notes with what other people see.

I have found that there are many different interpretations of this image. How is it possible to look at the same exact picture and arrive at completely different meanings from it? Our brains make instant decisions based on patterns it has established from our own lived experiences. Because we have different lived experiences, our context is unique, and we all see the world differently, which is a good thing. I love this activity because it allows us to re-examine the artwork and see the perspective of someone else. It usually takes a minute or two, a conscious effort, and then the light bulb goes off and people see the viewpoints of someone else. This exercise isn't limited to interpreting artwork. It can be applied in many different situations so that we can better understand and, more importantly, hear one another's perspectives.

There is no us vs. them; there is just a collective us.

The minute we judge people who are different from us, we dismiss their humanity. To open up your perspectives, consider comparing notes with somebody very different from you. Someone you also have a high degree of trust or rapport with. Please keep in mind, we never want to ask people different from us to educate us on what it's like to be them.

Here are some questions to get the conversation started:

- What were your experiences like growing up?
- How have your experiences shaped who you are?
- What is something you wish people knew about you?

- What challenges do you experience?
- What is one way someone could be helpful if they wanted to be a better ally?

This should feel like a conversation, not an interview. There is no script. The only way to empathize with others different from you is to learn more about them. While there are no guarantees this will work, we do know, with exposure over time, our empathy muscles strengthen. It's hard to categorize someone or "other" people once you understand them better. You humanize them.

Othering means to make someone feel less than because they are a part of an underrepresented group.

Othering could be asking someone where they are from (because they are not White) or assuming they have certain skills or interests based on their association with a group—any curious, yet harmful questions that single someone out and make them feel they are not a part of the group. Well-intentioned people say these things all the time. Just compare notes with a person of color if you are White or an LGBTQ+ identifying person if you are straight and cisgender or with a person with disabilities if you are non-disabled. These "othering" experiences happen much more often than people in the majority group realize.

As allies, it's always important to do our homework first. For example, you can sit down with somebody you know who is of a different race, ethnicity, cultural background, religious background, socioeconomic status, sexual orientation, ability, or gender identity with the intention to better understand them. That's the goal. The goal is not to impart your thoughts, not to share your story. Empathy is putting our egos aside.

I have had my share of mishaps by making conversations about me as an ally, especially when I'm in protector mode, experiencing the expert effect, or wanting to stay in control. Some techniques that have helped me counteract these impulses are:

- **Slow down your brain.** Your brain is working overtime and processing lots of information without your knowledge. Take deep breaths, walk off the energy, and focus on the other person fully.
- **Pause your judgment.** It is impossible to fully turn off our brain's love of categorization. It can be shifted for small pieces of conversations. Awkward silences are okay. It demonstrates you are listening.
- **Reframe.** Rather than fall into the trap of making it about you, keep shifting it back to the person you are talking to. What is different about their situation? What do you not understand?
- **Ask open-ended questions.** Most people think they ask more open-ended questions than they actually do. We love to test our assumptions with closed-ended questions. Ask questions you truly don't know the answers to.
- **Listen more than speak.** When we listen, we learn. When we speak, we hear what we already know. Take an inventory at the end of an empathetic conversation on listening vs. speaking.

When people share hard things with you, rarely do they want your advice, judgment, or to hear a story about a time when it happened to you. They really just want to be listened to. Think about the last time you went through something hard personally. Did you want someone to give you advice about how to handle it? Did you want someone to tell you a story about a time when that happened to them? Did you want someone to feel sorry for you?

As human beings, we are wired for connection and belonging. As Maslow first said back in 1942, Once our basic physiological needs are met with food and water, and our physical needs of safety are met, we seek connection. We have a primal need to be accepted, to be seen, and to belong in all spaces of our lives.

> *We don't stay in places where we don't feel like we belong.*

Not Sympathy

Empathy is the ability to identify and understand another person's situation without judgment, the full acceptance of their story. You have not lived their situation to be able to relate to it. Sympathy, by contrast, is projecting a feeling of less than (looking down upon) on someone for the hardship they are experiencing.

> *"If you judge people, you have no time to love them." Mother Teresa*

As allies-in-training, here are some well-intentioned statements to avoid:

- "I had that happen too"
- "Bless your heart"
- "You poor thing"
- "How can I help?"

Instead, consider these statements to show you really want to empathize:

- "I am sorry"
- "I have no idea how you feel"
- "That sounds hard"

- "Let me help you by ___."

When someone is experiencing pain, they rarely know what help they need or what support should look like for them.

Being an ally is like being a soft place for someone to land.

I was in my early twenties when my mom died. A lot of people felt sorry for me. A lot of people were there for the first month after she died. But as time passed, fewer people checked on me, and when they would, it was usually with a sad look on their face, like I was someone to be pitied. I didn't know what kind of support or help I needed at the time nor how to cope with my emotions. I now realize that it was my allies who would invite me to go out to dinner and listen, send me inspirational quotes, and drop by with coffee for a chat who helped me get through such a dark and lonely time in my life.

People who are experiencing the adversity of diversity don't know what support looks like. If they did, they wouldn't be in that situation. Allies do the guesswork for the person in need and think about what they might need and align It with what they are able to provide. For example, what hobbies or interests does the person have? Are they time-deprived and need help with meals or errands? Are you good at cooking, shopping, or do you enjoy things that they enjoy? Find the synergy of what they need and what you can provide and meet them where they're at.

After George Floyd was murdered in the summer of 2020, I was unsure of what to say to my friends of color, or if I should say anything at all. So, I kept quiet for the first few days, and now I realize that I was completely wrong. By the time I reached out and asked them how they were doing, they'd already heard from all of their White friends, and I was just another White person asking them to help me understand their pain. I felt that I was adding to their burden. Now I am mindful to reach out to them when there are events that are triggering in the news cycle about diversity.

Even with my experience in DEI training, when I look at a picture of a person of color experiencing trauma, it's through my own White lens. I feel empathy, but I don't feel like the trauma is happening to me and people like me. For people of color, it's like seeing a mirror of them experiencing the trauma they all too often see in our news cycle and in our flawed criminal justice system. After the events of the summer of 2020, the popularity of allyship increased, but there was still a lack of real action. I asked my friends of color, "What should I do?" Most commonly, they said, keep talking, keep showing up in your spaces of influence.

People who are experiencing the adversity of diversity want us to keep talking.

My friend and ally, Liesel, is an empathy trainer. She and I were at a gathering recently and she asked me a very curious question. "What did you learn most about yourself from the pandemic?"

Her question stopped me mid-bite. It was such a genuinely empathetic question that I had to really think about my response. I couldn't simply answer with a quick one-word response. I had to pause and really think about it. She commanded a real response.

As I paused and thought about the answer to the question, she continued to nibble on her food, maintain healthy eye contact, and show that she really wanted to hear the answer. She wasn't trying to stump me. She wasn't trying to one-up me. I knew she genuinely was curious. What was beautiful was that she was modeling exactly what she teaches without going into teaching mode.

I responded that my partner and I fell in love again during the pandemic. That we spent so much time together as a family and realized how lucky we were to have shared interests and things to connect on. She followed up with more empathetic questions, asking about details I had shared in my response: What shared interests did we have? What did we connect on?

As allies, we don't know what we don't know.

I had been feeling terrible that night with the stress of my new baby not feeling well, wanting to be present for my friends, and feeling overwhelmed. Liesel helped me feel seen and heard. She made me feel like I belonged there. That's the magic of empathy. When done intentionally and consistently, people extend their trust to you. You learn things you didn't know before. You build bridges to people you don't naturally understand. You maybe even learn how wrong you were about somebody you had prejudged without knowing that well.

Paradox

DEI conversations are very ambiguous in nature. When I compare notes with other DEI practitioners, we often compare stories of paradox. There is no right or wrong, Black or White. There is instead lots of grey area and room for error. You can be right and wrong at the same time. Vulnerability and shame researcher and thought leader, Brené Brown, found in her leadership research that embracing paradox is one of the most distinguishable traits of leaders. It separates the good leaders from the average leaders.

DEI requires us to embrace the tension of opposites. If we enter conversations thinking there's only room for one answer, we leave no room for other answers. Young people are quite good at holding the tension of paradox. They understand, for instance, that colors can be mixed together to make other colors on a color palette, that someone doesn't have to identify exclusively as a boy or girl, or that someone with a disability can do things that someone who is non-disabled cannot do.

DEI is a "both and" conversation.

When we get stuck on who's right and who's wrong, we lose sight of the bigger goal. DEI is intended to bring all voices together collectively. One of the only downsides to DEI is that it can take teams longer times to make decisions. Let's be clear, those decisions are eighty-seven percent better and, in a business setting, likely to double your revenue and profitability rates. DEI does take time because we have to acknowledge the different perspectives, we have to hear ideas that we may have never heard before, and we have to be open to doing things differently than we have before.

Diversity means doing things differently.

The definition of insanity is doing the same thing, over and over, and expecting a different result. A lot of times we do things unconsciously that have been modeled for us by previous generations. We're in fact just parroting the same phrases, going through the same motions, doing the same things that we were taught, because it's easier. You can't have inclusion and do things the same way when historically there has been a lack of diversity. This is why the paradox is so powerful.

Cognitive dissonance describes our brain's difficulty processing two seemingly competing pieces of information at the same time. Our brains don't like paradoxes. Our brains like certainty. Once we first learn something, unlearning it or replacing it with new information is very difficult to do. This creates significant barriers for those who were taught to be colorblind, to just appreciate differences but not talk about the real issues of racism, homophobia, sexism, and other dimensions of difference.

Like many others growing up in the Midwest, I was taught US History several times. First in eighth grade, a second time in eleventh grade, and again in junior year of college. Each time I learned the exact same narrative about a group of White men creating a place where we were "all equal." I did not learn about any leaders of color (except for the stereotypical, well-known names), women, people with disabilities, or those who identified as LGBTQ+.

I now know I was programmed to believe in the myth of meritocracy (hard work pays off) and an apathy towards those who didn't try as hard. Most of us don't know what we don't know, and I have found that it is really difficult to re-learn concepts learned in my childhood as a middle-aged adult. I've had to do a lot of self-education to unlearn those harmful messages that I learned several times during the pivotal years of my life. Replacing existing information in our brains with new, conflicting information is not easy. It takes practice and, even then, repetition to rewire the brain.

This next generation should not have to do that amount of work. They should be taught about all people throughout history, the major mistakes we made as a society, and not to oversimplify and whitewash our history with the message that "things are better now". When people grow up hearing those messages over and over again, they believe them. It makes it harder to understand the importance of DEI and doing things differently if you think the ways of the past are idealized.

If we don't learn our full history, we are bound to repeat it.

A few years ago, I posted a picture of a Dr. Seuss quote on Instagram about curiosity and included the hashtag "diversity and inclusion." Many commented that Dr. Seuss was a racist and should never be associated with the words diversity and inclusion. This was before several problematic books featuring stereotypical images and harmful phrasing were withdrawn. At the time, I did not know about this. I only had two Dr. Seuss books at home and thought their messages were inclusive, although not diversely represented. I did my research and sure enough I was wrong to use the hashtag "diversity and inclusion." This story illustrates paradox and cognitive dissonance that accompanies it. When we associate Dr. Seuss exclusively as a racist, it leaves no room for some of the books to not be racist. It's hard to hold space for those two truths.

Recently, I commented on a LinkedIn post with a picture of two Black male NBA players kneeling during the national anthem with their White teammate standing beside them. All three were touching one another in solidarity. The image alone is paradoxical. The comment I made was that this was a great example of paradox and embracing the "yes and" in the conversation. My understanding was that, as a White player, he wanted to support his teammates and also respect members of his family who were in the military and didn't feel comfortable kneeling, therefore he stood with them.

The White player had a Black Lives Matter shirt on and appeared in the photo to be supportive of his teammates.

His Black teammates were embracing him and his show of support. It certainly is thought-provoking and difficult to hold the tension of those opposites. Shame and blame aren't going to bring anyone into the conversation about DEI. The response to my comment surprised me. People said everything from, "This is such a typical White person response" to how inappropriate and insensitive my comments were about the Black Lives Matter movement. Again, holding the tension of opposites and paradox, is it possible to believe that the White player was showing his support in his own way?

There is no right or wrong answer here. You're absolutely one hundred percent entitled to your opinion. I see this as a "both and" moment and I'll continue to look for those moments, especially when tensions are high. If we both sit in our prospective corners and are unwilling to listen to each other, or meet in the middle, DEI work will remain slow and tedious. Allies say "yes and" when they disagree with someone. They model paradoxical behavior. They ask if conflicting situations are "both and" opportunities.

Each chapter has a short assessment to better understand where you are and where you want to be as an ally. Consider the assessment results today as your starting point on your ally journey before moving forward with another ally skill set.

Assessment:

☐ **People share hard things with me.**

- ☐ I like learning new things about people.
- ☐ I focus my attention on others in the conversation.
- ☐ I can easily embrace two seemingly opposite points of view.
- ☐ I listen first instead of trying to problem-solve for someone else.
- ☐ People seek out my input on hard decisions.
- ☐ I am recognized for being a good listener.
- ☐ I get energy from others' stories.
- ☐ I resist making conversations about me and my experiences.
- ☐ I deeply understand that my lived experiences are very different from others.

Empathy Reader Activity

Self-Reflection and Practice with Empathy

1. Watch the <u>Brené Brown on Sympathy vs. Empathy video</u> (To find this video, do a search on YouTube for '*Brené Brown sympathy empathy*').

2. Reflect on these questions through journaling or discussing with a trusted person in your life:

   a. What situations/circumstances/people groups are easier for you to empathize with? (For example, you may be able to empathize with someone who battles chronic illness because you do as well.)

   b. What situations/circumstances/people groups often elicit a sympathetic response from you rather than an empathetic response? Why do you think that is?

   c. What is difficult about practicing empathy in your relationships? What about with strangers?

3. Practice. Keep these simple questions "in your back pocket" to help you empathize with others or start conversations that will elicit an empathetic connection.

a. "How are you *really* doing with
_____?" (situation, circumstance,
relationship, event, etc.)

b. "What has been on your mind
lately?" Another way to word it may
be, "What has been causing you the
most stress lately?"

c. "What do you wish people
understood about you, your
situation, your life, etc.?"

Empathy Group or Family Activity

Materials:
- The following images (printed or on given slideshow):
    - <u>Perspective</u> (To find images, do a Google search for 'duck or rabbit image' or 'inkblot images')

Directions:
1. Show each of the images to the group and give the directions: "Look at this image and don't tell me what you see just yet. Just look at it and we will share what we see."
2. Show each image for about thirty seconds.
3. Ask: "What do you see?"
4. Make sure each person gets a chance to answer. Point out similarities and differences between what each child sees. Let them openly react to the differences between what they see.

Say:
"Isn't it interesting how we can all look at the same picture but see completely different things? Why do you think it is that we see different things? Is it a bad thing that we see different things? Is there one right way to see things? Explain."

"How does this apply to looking at people around us? What makes us see people differently?"

"What happens when we see people differently? How are you seeing this play out in the world today?"

CHAPTER THREE: VULNERABILITY

If vulnerability were easy, we would all be doing it. As someone who practices vulnerability, I acknowledge its difficulty, but this skill is critical for DEI conversations at home.

Because we're a product of our lived experiences, we don't understand what it's like to be somebody different from us. That's why understanding your patterns, your ally why, and practicing empathy are all helpful steps on the ally journey. The next skill set is a more sensitive area for most, being vulnerable.

How comfortable do you feel being vulnerable with others?

This answer likely depends. You probably feel comfortable or even safe being vulnerable with some members of your family, your closest friends, or the people you've known for a long time. That's because you can probably predict their behavior because you've had enough experiences with them to know that you can trust them to show the vulnerable side of yourself.

The challenge is that when we don't know the other person, or we don't understand their lived experiences, vulnerability becomes increasingly difficult. DEI conversations are filled with these types of experiences. People who experience other dimensions of diversity will not have as much in common with us by default (although there's likely a lot of commonalities that don't appear initially). It's harder to be vulnerable with people you don't know well or don't know how to predict if it is safe to be vulnerable with.

All humans naturally have affinity bias. Affinity bias is a form of unconscious bias that we are rarely aware of. For our own survival, we naturally gravitate towards people like us. As a tribal species, ninety percent of our human history was spent hunting and gathering before the recent settling that came with agriculture some twelve thousand years ago. Before that, we were surrounded by people who looked like us. We could easily identify who were members of our tribe, or part of another tribe, based on their appearance. Given the global world we now all live in, clearly this is no longer true.

> *Vulnerability is putting yourself out there without the expectation of reciprocation.*

Vulnerability is necessary when having conversations with people who don't look like us, behave like us, or seem to have a lot in common with us. That is precisely why vulnerability is hard. It is in our survival, our fight-or-flight wiring, to not trust those who do not look or behave like us. Vulnerability doesn't mean taking life-or-death risks; it is freely admitting mistakes, showing signs of weakness, saying "I don't know," or asking for feedback and really wanting to hear it.

Vulnerability-Based Trust

There's no way to predict when it's safe to be vulnerable. You can't plan a vulnerability time block on your calendar. You can't script a vulnerable conversation with your family, but you can model vulnerability and hope that others follow suit and accept that they might not.

Vulnerability is a choice, a necessary choice for DEI to work.

It is impossible to be supportive of someone different from you if you're not willing to be vulnerable. Vulnerability and trust are necessary for a healthy ally relationship. If you have a low level of vulnerability, you likely have a low degree of trust. When you have a high amount of trust, you likely have a strong ability to be vulnerable in the relationship.

"Remember teamwork begins by building trust. And the only way to do that is to overcome our need for invulnerability." Patrick Lencioni

Several years ago, when I first started my DEI training business, I pursued my Master Coach Certification. As part of the process, we had to learn a new way of communicating to shift from an advice-giving mindset to promoting a self-discovery mindset (more on coaching in Chapter Seven). I thought that I had it all figured out, but I quickly realized during our role play exercises that I did not. I asked a lot of leading questions, I tested a lot of my assumptions, and I centered myself in the conversation too often. I had to unlearn a lot of unhelpful behaviors that had taken root in me as a child and into adulthood. Putting myself out there, with the potential to fail, felt very vulnerable.

The instructor for our class used the phrase "dancing in the dark" to describe the experience of learning new things as an adult. I still think about this when I resist being vulnerable and struggle to put myself out there, even though I know it's the right thing to do. For me, dancing in the dark is letting someone else blindly take the lead and then taking turns following each other's lead, even though you don't know where you're going. You may not be sure what the final outcome will be, or how others around you are perceiving the dance, but you're dancing nonetheless.

DEI is a vulnerable dance in the dark.

I would be remiss if I did not again mention Brené Brown, researcher and thought leader on vulnerability and shame. She has an infamous story in her book, *Rising Strong*, recounting the time she wore a Speedo. She described a time when she and her husband, Steve, were taking a swim in a lake together and she was in her Speedo. She was proud to be what she called "rocking her Speedo," but to her dismay, Steve did not seem to notice. The story she was telling herself, that she calls the Shitty First Draft (SFD), was that he did not like her Speedo. She later discovered that he was simply focused on the task at hand, swimming, and wasn't thinking about her and her Speedo. It wasn't about her.

We often think people are thinking about us more than they actually are. We think that everyone is out to get us. If only they understood us better, or recognized us for all the things that we're doing, we would feel validated. The problem is that most people are doing the same thing. They are thinking about themselves. The key with vulnerability is accepting it is not about you, and whatever SFD is playing in your mind is likely to be untrue. If we put our cards on the table, others will likely follow suit. Vulnerability is rarely met with a lack of vulnerability.

When your vulnerability is not reciprocated, there could be a few potential reasons. Most often, the other party feels insecure about their lack of knowledge or experience in the conversation. The antidote is finding out what information the person needs to better understand the subject or what might help them become more curious.

Another reason is a lack of trust. Trust has a reciprocal relationship with vulnerability, so to build trust is to build the vulnerability muscle.

"It is not the critic who counts; not the man who points out how the strong man stumbles, or where the doer of deeds could have done them better. The credit belongs to the man who is actually in the arena, whose face is marred by dust and sweat and blood; who strives valiantly; who errs, who comes short again and again, because there is no effort without error and shortcoming; but who does actually strive to do the deeds; who knows great enthusiasms, the great devotions; who spends himself in a worthy cause; who at the best knows in the end the triumph of high achievement, and who at the worst, if he fails, at least fails while daring greatly, so that his place shall never be with those cold and timid souls who neither know victory nor defeat." Teddy Roosevelt

One exercise I love to do during my DEI training with organizations is to have everyone pull out a piece of paper and list the people in their life they admire the most. Then, I have them think about the common traits that they share and prioritize a basket of three to five common traits. It is highly likely that the words trust, vulnerability, authenticity, or some form of these words will appear on the list.

Who do you trust and why?

Matching and Mirroring

As social creatures, we are wired to fit in, to belong. We're not meant to survive on our own; we're meant to survive in large groups. For our survival over time, we have leveraged the talents from different members of our group to maximize outcomes for the group. Different skill sets helped us all be better collectively. What we have in common are our values and beliefs. As groups, we tend to align and have similar values and beliefs so that we make decisions that are congruent and keep our group cohesive. Given this need to align, humans are naturally wired to match and mirror what they see in front of them. That means we tend to take on the behaviors of those we spend the most time with.

I remember the summer between middle school and high school, I spent every waking hour with my best friend. Our parents joked that we were attached at the hip. At the end of that summer, I almost had an identity crisis going back to school thinking, *I'm not going to be with her all the time. How will I even know how to act or behave?* We had synced up our body language, jokes, bedtimes, the foods we ate, even our menstrual cycles.

It has long been human nature to sync up with those you're around, because if you are attacked or experience a crisis, it is important to be able to predict the behavior of others around you. The same goes for vulnerability. When someone displays vulnerability, rarely do people not match and mirror that vulnerability, although you can't expect that reciprocation to happen one hundred percent of the time. I have found anecdotally in my research, with clients' experiences and in my own experiences, that ninety-eight percent of the time people match and mirror vulnerability.

Of course, there are times when people don't match and mirror vulnerability. Our brains remember these negative experiences far more than the positive ones, although fortunately, they are generally less frequent. My negative experience was with a former colleague, let's call her Helen. It was early on in my business, and I was pretty uncertain if it was going to work out. I didn't have a lot of clients, I wasn't effective in my marketing, and my sales process was a mess. I still had a lack of confidence in myself and my ability to do something that I hadn't done before.

In hindsight, I was definitely suffering from imposter syndrome (not believing in yourself despite evidence to support achievement), but I didn't know what that was at the time. I found someone I thought would be a great mentor, Helen. I reached out to her, scheduled a time to talk, and we sat down and had a lovely conversation about the things she had learned over the years. She had been speaking, training, and consulting for over thirty years and was a well-known expert in my local area.

I remember sharing the challenges I was having with her. I had one client who was giving me a lot of work but was requiring a lot of travel away from my family. I shared that it might be best to pivot towards more local work. The look on her face told me everything I needed to know about Helen. She instantly grimaced and said, "Have you ever thought about quitting your business? Maybe it's not meant to be?"

Rather than matching and mirroring, she got defensive. Perhaps she was insecure about me competing with her in our local market and so she planted seeds of doubt in my mind. I felt defeated and upset. I didn't know what to do. Luckily, I had many other allies around me who helped me see my potential when I couldn't see it in myself. That's the beauty of allies. They see things in us that we have yet to see in ourselves.

Allies hold up the mirror for us to see how beautiful and capable we are, even if we haven't done the things that make us special yet.

When leading with vulnerability, you will experience comfort with discomfort. It's like a muscle you have to remember to flex. It never feels fully safe because it isn't, but the rewards of being vulnerable outweigh the risks. Every time I think about being vulnerable, I sweat a little bit, but leaning into that discomfort does get easier with practice.

"We redefine what it means to be a good person as someone who is trying to be better, as opposed to someone who is allowing themselves to believe in the illusion that they are always a good person." Dolly Chugh

Vulnerability is less about getting it right and more about showing someone our imperfections and then, together, getting it right. If we are trying to be perfect, we cannot be vulnerable.

Shame Triggers

Most people avoid vulnerability because of the fear of the shame that often accompanies it. Think of shame as a passenger in the car driven by vulnerability. It's hard to put yourself out there and be vulnerable and imperfect without feeling a little bit of a knock to your ego. Shame is that negative feeling of stress, or sometimes humiliation, that often comes with vulnerability.

According to *Psychology Today*,[13] extinction, mutilation, loss of autonomy, separation, and ego death are the top five basic human fears. We are born with only two fears— fear of falling and of loud noises. These fears can prevent us from being fully vulnerable with one another. If people

---

[13] Albrecht, "The (Only) Five Fears We All Share."

feel the risk of entering the diversity conversation because of the shame that could come with it, then they're unlikely to be a part of the very conversation they need to be a part of. Many well-intentioned folks who fall into the majority group feel like they might say or do the wrong thing in the DEI conversation and therefore avoid it. They avoid the potential shame that could accompany that kind of vulnerability.

Shame and blame are not vehicles for social justice.

If the majority group is afraid of being involved in the conversation, perhaps we should meet them where they're at. Figure out where their shame triggers could be and where our own triggers might lie. When shame meets shame, the results can be disastrous. As an ally, it's important to understand your own triggers as well as the triggers of others to be able to successfully manage them, especially in an emotional conversation.

I like to do this exercise with corporate leaders. Write down the things that embarrass you or scare you or elicit fear. Here are some starting ideas:

- Irrelevance
- Being called a racist/sexist/bad person
- Making mistakes
- Not having the answer
- Being wrong
- Having to unlearn or relearn something
- Reckoning with discomfort
- Fumbling in uncertainty
- Lack of clear path forward
- Offending someone

Chances are these all-too-common fears, which are necessary to confront in a DEI conversation, will prevent us from talking openly about diversity. When entering conversations with children, friends, and family, these fears will express themselves. As an ally, empathize with the fear someone else might be feeling. Self-proclaim your own fear. Manage the fear in the moment and know it comes with uncharted territory.

> *When we understand and confront our own fears as allies, we model for others that it is safe to be vulnerable.*

Reflect again on the opening question in the chapter: How comfortable do you feel being vulnerable with others? Each chapter has a short assessment to better understand where you are and where you want to be as an ally. Consider these assessment results before moving forward with another ally skill set.

Assessment:

- ☐ **I feel comfortable being vulnerable with others different from myself.**
- ☐ **I admit when I make mistakes.**
- ☐ **I am okay not having all of the answers.**
- ☐ **I trust others different from myself.**
- ☐ **I embrace the opportunity to learn new information.**
- ☐ **I seek out opportunities where I am uncomfortable.**
- ☐ **I fumble with uncertainty.**
- ☐ **I accept ambiguity.**

- ☐ **I am okay knowing not everyone will mirror my vulnerability.**
- ☐ **I seek feedback, even when it is hard.**

Vulnerability Reader Activity

Shame Triggers Exercise

1.   In order for us to show up vulnerably, we need to recognize where shame can keep us hiding from vulnerable moments. Take a look at the list below. Circle the ones that can or have been a shame trigger for you:

     a. Irrelevance
     b. Being called a racist/sexist/bad person
     c. Making mistakes
     d. Not having the answers
     e. Being wrong
     f. Having to unlearn or relearn something
     g. Reckoning with discomfort
     h. Rumbling in uncertainty
     i. Lacking a clear path forward
     j. Ticking someone off

2. Reflect on where these triggers show up for you (conversations, situations, relationships, etc.)

3. Grab a journal or piece of paper. Write down your top three shame triggers on the left side of the paper. On the right side, write down the truth and/or an action that will help you to manage that shame trigger so that you can show up vulnerably for yourself and other people.

Example:
Making mistakes causes me to feel shame. No one is perfect and everyone is learning. I am allowed to make mistakes and learn from them so that I can move forward. When I make a mistake, I am willingly showing others that I am not perfect and that I am learning too. That gives people the space to make mistakes around

me. This creates a space for vulnerability and authenticity, which creates connection.

Vulnerability Group or Family Activity

Materials:
- -Blank paper
- -Coloring utensils

Directions:
1. Hand each group member a piece of paper and coloring utensils.
2. Say: "Draw a picture of a leader." Do not give extra directions or context. Let them go with the prompt based on their own thoughts.
3. Ask:
    a. "Why did you draw what you did?"
    b. "Why did you choose that race/skin color for a leader?"
    c. "Why did you choose that gender for a leader?"
    d. "Why is your leader wearing that?"
4. As you discuss the answers to these questions, you may begin uncovering biases or prejudices that people have against certain genders, races, socioeconomic backgrounds, etc. Allow them to have a safe space to talk about their biases and start to discuss how those biases can change. If you don't know what to say, continue to ask "why" questions to get them to explain their thinking.

Say:
"I'm glad we got to do this together. Even though we realized that we have some negative views of certain kinds of people, we were able to be honest and open and share without the fear of judgment. Now that it's in the

open, we can learn to think differently. Anyone can be a leader. We might not have come to that conclusion if we hadn't had this open conversation together."

CHAPTER FOUR: CURIOSITY

Curiosity did not kill the cat. Curiosity is essential for those who hope to be allies. As children, we are naturally curious about the world around us. We ask a lot more questions than claim to have answers. As we age, we tend to slowly lose this curiosity. As we get older, it becomes harder to imagine the world being different than how we have experienced it. We have a knack for saying things like, "That's just the way it is," or "That's the way we've always done it," when questioned about the status quo.

The status quo is the antithesis of diversity. To eradicate the status quo, we must be curious and open our minds up to new possibilities and new ways of doing things. Curiosity is shifting the mindset from "what I know" to "what I wish I knew." It's understanding that "I don't have all the answers, but that is a good thing." It's an opportunity to learn, instead of the fear of being wrong or the risk of saying, "I don't know."

Curiosity is the gap between what you know and what you want to know.

Curiosity is one of the ally skills that we can lean on our kids to help us with as adults. We can follow their lead. Watch how they stay curious in the face of uncertainty and adversity. Instead of locking in on one answer, they're more willing to consider a vast array of possibilities. Their minds stay open to new possibilities because they have not experienced as many negative experiences as adults generally do. Research has shown that the more time adults spend with children, the more their curiosity rubs off on us.

This is why vulnerability and curiosity go hand in hand. As adults, it's difficult for us to let go of control and risk not knowing the answers, especially in a delicate conversation like DEI. If curiosity elicits fear for you, ask yourself, "What's the worst that could happen? What could I learn from this? What is possible?"

One of the compulsions we have, especially as caregivers and parents, is to advise our children. Adults love to tell children what to do when they're dealing with adversity. Last year, my six-year-old daughter was dealing with a bullying situation in school. She would come home with unpleasant stories about what had happened to her and her friends that day.

At first, I jumped right into advising mode. As I was telling her what to say and do, she would look at me wild-eyed and overwhelmed with my adult advice. After a few attempts to solve her problem for her, she finally told me that she did not think that would work. That was my "aha" moment. Taking a cue from her bewilderment as a chance to be better, I began reframing my approach to her problems with, "Is this a situation where you want me to give you advice or you want me to listen?" Now, ninety percent of the time she answers that question with, "I just want you to listen, Mom." My job as a parent just got a lot easier by simply staying curious.

Curiosity requires a lot of energy. It's hard to stay in the curious mindset for a long time. The brain desires certainty and avoids ambiguity. If you find this difficult, be sure to give yourself a break. Like many of the skills detailed in this book, with practice, curiosity will get easier for you. Take a walk, meditate, shift gears to another task, and come back to something that requires your curious energy. Often, just holding the curious mindset for a few more minutes, or even a few more seconds, can do wonders for the realm of possibilities.

Allies stay curious a little longer.

Bias Prevents Us from Curiosity

Our brains love categories and form biases based on categories from a young age. When our brains evaluate stimuli (people, objects) the brain makes snap judgments about them. It places objects into categories based on past experiences and makes automatic associations with people. This is helpful for everyday, innocent interactions like recognizing your neighbor or using shortcuts like a uniform to identify the person as a healthcare worker or police officer. It becomes a challenge when we make assumptions that are not true about someone, for example, because of their skin color, gender, or disability.

Many of the dimensions of diversity are not visible or apparent. In some parts of the world, an estimated seventy to eighty percent of disabilities are not visible to the naked eye[14]. LGBTQ+ identity is rarely able to be detected based on visible traits or interactions. Gender identity and race are also extremely fluid and are spectrums rather than binaries. Increasingly people identify as multi-racial and gender nonbinary. Yet our primitive brains still make these automatic assumptions based on binary, outdated categories.

Unconscious biases, or implicit biases, are attitudes that are held subconsciously and affect the way individuals feel and think about others around them.

---

[14] Royal Bromtom and Harefield Hospitals, "More Than Meets the Eye."

Having bias does not make you a bad person. It makes you human. Although expressing bias is not an excuse for bad behavior, we are all still accountable for our behavior, even when bias is at play.

One hundred percent of people have biases some of the time.

A microaggression is when we act in a way that reflects our bias. "Micro" because they're seemingly small; "aggression" because they hurt. The thing with microaggressions is they are like death by a thousand paper cuts. They are the sum of the negative experiences that take a toll on someone. It is not the individual instance where someone assumes that you are not the leader, or you're not being included in meetings, constantly being interrupted, or someone else taking credit for your ideas, but instead the overall impact of each of those microaggressions happening at different points in a day, week, or a month. The cumulative impact of these negative experiences can be exhausting.

Microaggressions are the unintentional, often subtle signals to someone that indicate they don't belong.

I went on a road trip out west a few summers back with my daughter. We camped out at national parks. One morning we woke up covered in mosquito bites. We had not noticed the few bites we had gotten the night before, but when we woke up covered from head to toe, we were both in immense pain. Microaggressions are like mosquito bites. The first one itches, and as you get more and more, it becomes more overwhelming and becomes harder to resist the need to itch. It's the cumulative effect of all of the microaggressions that cause the pain, not the one individual one (although those can hurt too).

In the book *Blind Spot*, authors Anthony Greenwald and Mahzarin Banaji[15] use the Harvard Implicit Association Test to measure biases on key diversity dimensions. Here's how the data breaks down by diversity dimension:

- Age: ninety-six percent of people prefer younger to older people.
- Race: eighty-six percent of people associate Black with oppression and White with power.
- Gender: ninety-five percent of people associate women with caregiving and men with providing.

Bias can be a barrier to curiosity. If you're making assumptions about someone without the information to support it, your curiosity will be hindered. The starting point is self-awareness. Take an inventory of your biases for free and anonymously with the proven pattern recognition tool at implicit.harvard.edu. While the assessment is not perfect, it helps people understand where their biases might lie, and with awareness over time, behaviors can shift. It is hard to change behavior if we are not self-aware.

Non-inclusive behavior is rooted in our lived experiences. Lived experiences often dictate our biases. To help identify the origins of your bias, take an inventory of your lived experiences during your childhood and adulthood.

- How many people of color did you know growing up?
- How many people in the LGBTQ+ community are in your family or friends circle?

---

[15] Harvard Implicit Bias Test

- How many people did you know with disabilities as you were growing up?

Seventy-five percent of White people live in White-dominant communities.

Exposure to differences will not solve the problem alone. Bias is everywhere. It's in our media, our education, and lives through our friends and family circles. One way to lead like an ally at home is to intentionally expose your friends and family to different cultures and new ideas. This can be done through learning and celebrating different cultural holidays, learning about and eating foods of different ethnicities and cultures, and inviting people of different cultures into your home (when appropriate).

There are lots of different types of families.

Diversity goes beyond race and gender. It's important that we emphasize in our messages to children that there are different types of families. Some families have two moms or two dads, some families have a Black mom and a White dad, or a biracial parent, or caregiver with a disability. Often the White, straight, cisgender, non-disabled standard is normalized as what a family looks like. Children's storybooks reinforce this narrative with protagonists largely being White, straight, non-disabled males. In fact, there are more animals in children's books than kids of color total. Diversify your bookshelf and showcase stories of all types of people.

According to the Cooperative Children's Book Center, in 2018, children's book characters were:

- Fifty percent White
- Twenty-seven percent animals
- Twenty-three percent kids of color

Although movies have gotten much better with diverse representation in recent years, there is still a lag. Seventy-two percent of films have White male protagonists. That means that children of color, girls, or LGBTQ+ kids and kids with disabilities are unlikely to see themselves reflected in movies. They have an extra challenge to put themselves in the shoes of someone who is not like them. Meanwhile, White boys grow up seeing themselves mirrored and represented in virtually all facets of their life. They feel like spaces belong to them because they see people like them leading and being central to the narrative.

The Bechdel test is a great tool to use to find diverse representation in films by gender. It has three simple questions that can be reframed for race, LGBTQ+, disability, or other dimensions of diversity.

1. At least two women are featured.
2. The women talk to each other.
3. The women talk about something other than men.

According to the Bechdel Test website,[16] only fifty-six percent of films in their database pass all three tests. Seeing yourself reflected is important. When we don't see diverse representation and inclusive behavior modeled in our culture, it allows the myth of meritocracy to permeate. We often assume that people have the same set of conditions that we did growing up and in our current state. The idea of the myth of meritocracy is that hard work pays off for all. However, in reality, the starting point is different for people of color, girls, those who identify as LGBTQ+, and people with disabilities. This concept is embedded in our culture and is false. Hard work looks

---

[16] Bechdel Test Movie List

different for people based on the conditions of their lived experiences.

Stop telling people to pull themselves up by their bootstraps. We don't all have bootstraps.

Lastly, our brain is wired for quick decision-making. We tend not to spend a lot of time thinking about decisions. We like what's familiar, comfortable, and usually go with our gut. We make decisions emotionally and justify them rationally later. That's why the subjects of bias and staying curious are intrinsically linked. Rather than making quick decisions, spend more time thinking about decisions before making them (a few seconds even) by rationally asking yourself some questions first. This can lead to a much more holistic mindset and a better decision. That's why the decisions made by diverse teams are so much more innovative and ultimately better than those made by teams that lack diversity.

Questions Help Us Stay Curious

To stay curious a little longer, consider asking yourself these questions:

- What is possible?
- What is the wildest idea we could come up with?
- What perspective are we missing?
- Who haven't we heard from?
- What skills do we want to learn?

It just takes one ally to signal to others the desire for diversity. Looking around a social event, dinner venue, or meeting and seeing a lack of diversity is an opportunity to speak up as an ally. Put up your ally radar and look for situations where diversity could be better. The mere question, "Who is not here, and why?" or "I would like to see more diversity in this (setting)," brings awareness for others to also be mindful about how diverse the event or setting is (or is not).

DEI is an intentional and consistent mindset.

The fear of looking silly or not knowing something prevents us from asking questions. Kids naturally ask a lot more questions than impart answers. While it can be exhausting as an adult with a young child to answer all of their questions, they're expressing their curious mindset naturally. The more we shut down their questions or refrain from being curious with them, the more they learn to not ask questions and make assumptions instead.

When I wrote my children's book "The Little Allies" in 2021, I originally wrote it to help kids have the conversation about diversity. However, I found that adults actually learned more from their children when they read it together. The children's curious questions indicated to them that they naturally see the world from a diverse perspective. It's through our conditioning and lived experiences that we start to unsee it and stop questioning behavior that's not inclusive. We only normalize non-inclusive behavior because of our constant exposure to the non-inclusive behavior in our media, culture, and our personal lives.

For example, why is Santa Claus almost always depicted as White? Why do we assume women are nurses instead of doctors? Why are most romance films about straight, non-disabled couples?

Choose Your Own Adventure

As a child who grew up in the 80s, I fondly remember the Choose Your Own Adventure books. At the end of each chapter, I could decide and flip ahead to the corresponding section in the book that matched my desired outcome. It was fun as a kid to feel empowered to co-create a story along with the author.

The same goes for being an ally at home. There is no one way to do this. It is a series of consistent, intentional actions that you select to focus on and over time demonstrate that you want to be an ally to others who are different from you.

It is not the responsibility of people who are different from you to educate you on what it's like to be them. You would never expect an architect to educate you on all their lived experiences and years of education about architecture. Or expect your doctor to explain the in-depth medical school lesson associated with your condition. The same goes for people who experience the adversity of diversity. You can absolutely lean on people with whom you have a trusting, deep relationship with to support you in your journey (if they've indicated they are willing), but they are not responsible for your education.

You are the only one responsible for your DEI education as an ally.

For us to get better at inclusion as a society, we must start with individually advocating for systemic change. It may feel like an uphill battle and that your individual actions do not amount to much change initially, but baby steps are steps and silence is compliance. Inaction is the same as accepting the status quo. So, ask yourself, if not for you, doesn't the next generation deserve better?

I recently had lunch with an ally of mine named Jeff. Jeff is a White man who is very passionate about history. He shared that he was surprised to learn some interesting facts about his own family's history in recent years. According to his findings, generations ago, members of his White family had been involved in coordinating the

Underground Railroad in the 1860s and had helped to engage White children in the civil rights efforts during the 1960s. He reflected candidly, "Why am I just now learning this?"

That's the challenge with DEI. All too often, the stories are kept concealed, not put on display, preventing future generations from learning from our history to be better in our future. Our brains are wired for stories. We learn more from stories than facts and figures. That is why children instinctively get excited during story time. We see ourselves as the characters in the story. In fact, it is a human survival technique to share stories to help younger generations learn from past generations' mistakes. Consider stories a vehicle for curiosity.

One important action step in allyship is to move away from silence and move towards action to learn about our real histories. Because history books are often written by the majority group, the spotlight is often on White, straight, cisgender men, and their perspectives, over time. Here are some history lessons that might be new for you:

- Black History: While slavery ended in 1865, almost immediately following, Jim Crow laws were implemented. These laws permitted lynching and the over-policing of Black people (in fact, the first known police force was the Slave Patrol). Redlining became common practice in the 1930s to protect White homeownership while simultaneously deeming BIPOC neighborhoods as too risky for bank loans. While the Fair Housing Act of 1968 was passed to fight the practice of redlining, the ripple effects of this discriminatory practice still continue today. Property is the biggest way to build generational wealth and still contributes to the wealth gap of ten times White to people of color today. Juneteenth and the Tulsa Massacre only recently became mainstream knowledge, and Black women did not have the right to vote until the Voting Rights Act of 1964.

- Native American History: While the idea of Thanksgiving is well-intentioned, that was the beginning of the end for native people in the United States. Today, Native Americans account for only one percent of the US population. They were called "savages" to justify mandated boarding schools for children and to promote unfair treatment. Native Americans were forced onto inhabitable land out west, where there is little water, infrastructure, or medical resources. Their mistreatment continues with cultural appropriation (sports mascots, dream catchers, references to powwows and totem poles). The Keystone Pipeline project today is problematic for Native Americans, as it continues to take advantage of Native Americans for the benefit of the majority group.

- Seventy-Year Women's Suffrage Story: While women did achieve the right to vote in 1920, the movement started much earlier, in the 1850s. The movement only benefited White women; women of color were highly involved at the onset and then were abandoned to appeal to White men supporting the movement. Many of the well-known women's suffrage leaders were not supportive of women of color.

- AAPI (Asian American Pacific Islander) History: From 1882 to 1952, the Chinese Exclusion Act prohibited Chinese laborers from entering the US workforce. One hundred twenty thousand Japanese Americans were forced into internment camps during WWII. More recently, during the

COVID pandemic, AAPI reported hate crimes have risen by forty-nine percent.

- LGBTQ+ History: Gay pride parades began in the 1970s shortly after the Stonewall Riots in NYC, bringing awareness to the community and allies. Since same-sex marriage finally became legal in 2015, social acceptance has tripled in support of the LGBTQ+ community. This is attributed to the engagement and support of advocates and allies.

- Disabilities History: An estimated one in four Americans identifies as having a disability, with the majority of those being non-apparent. It was only in 1990 that the Americans with Disabilities Act was passed to protect the basic rights of people with disabilities in the workplace. Many people with disabilities continue to be underemployed due to the lack of accommodations.

It may feel overwhelming to accept these facts if they are new to you. It was for me as well. It doesn't mean that we are bad people. It means we can learn from our history to be better in the future. If children continue to learn a history that depicts only the perspectives and experiences of White men, they most certainly will continue to support the status quo.

Real allies don't put the burden on those who are marginalized to educate them. Be curious to learn. There is no shortage of resources to support your learning journey as an ally. Choose a topic that interests you and dive in. Then dig into other areas. We have a fully vetted free resource list to learn more at NextPivot Point.com/resources to help you get started. If you cannot find a resource to support your learning, talk to people who you have a trusted relationship with. Start your inquiry with, "I am curious to learn more" or, "Help me understand." Be sure to let them know their time was valued and what you were able to learn because of their allyship.

Stay curious. Each chapter has a short assessment to better understand where you are and where you want to be as an ally. Consider these assessment results before moving forward with another ally skill set.

Assessment:

- ☐ I stay open to input.
- ☐ I ask, "What perspective are we missing?"
- ☐ I listen equally to all voices.
- ☐ I support new ideas without judgment.
- ☐ I say, "I am curious."
- ☐ I brainstorm new ways to solve old problems.
- ☐ I ask before I tell.
- ☐ I understand the real histories of DEI.
- ☐ I look for those who are not participating as an opportunity to engage.
- ☐ I research what I do not understand.

Curiosity Reader Activity

Bias Inventory

1. Take at least two assessments from the Harvard Implicit Association Test (To find this test, do a Google search for 'harvard implicit bias test').
2. What did you learn about your own biases?
3. What biases did you have that you didn't realize you had?
4. Where/how do you think these biases have formed in your life?
5. Compare notes with someone else. What shifted for both of you?

Curiosity Group or Family Activity

Materials:

      -All the toys and children's books in your house or group area (this can also be done by walking around a store such as Target or Walmart)

      -Blank piece of paper

      -Two different color writing utensils

Directions:

1. On the blank piece of paper, write down the following categories with room for tally marks: boy, girl, White, BIPOC, American, ethnic, non-disabled, disabled.

2. Choose one color writing utensil you will use for the books and a different color you will use for the toys.

3. Have group members gather all of the books.

4. Say: "We're going to try to find what different people groups are represented in our books. We have categories that we wrote on this paper. BIPOC means 'Black, Indigenous, and People of Color' and ethnic means someone who would be from a different country. We're going to flip through our books and put a tally for each category we see. Most of the time a character will get more than one tally. Like we might find a boy who is BIPOC and non-disabled, so we will give a tally for each category."

5. Work together to create your tallies.

6. Now, tell group members to gather all of their toys.

7. Do the same thing with their toys.

8. Sit together and look at the tallies.

Say:

"What are you noticing when you look at these tallies?"

"Why do you think that is?"

"Who seems to be missing from our toys and books?"

"Why do you think that is?"

"How can we change that?"

CHAPTER FIVE: EMOTIONS

As humans, we make decisions emotionally first and justify them rationally later. We like to think we're a lot more methodical than we actually are. Think about the last time you made a decision. Did you go with your gut? Did you take days to ruminate about it? Regardless of your decision-making speed, when you really think through the criteria used to make that decision, it probably had to do with your comfort level with the choice.

We are wired to make decisions that are comfortable. This creates a challenge with diversity and inclusion because, by nature, these decisions and conversations are not comfortable. They require us to get comfortable with the uncomfortable. Similar to the tools that we've talked about so far on the allyship journey at home, this is something that can be learned and flexed over time.

The first step is awareness. We need to be aware of the emotions we bring into conversations, our body language, the emotions of others, and the impact of our behavior on others. This might seem like a simplistic concept, yet in my work in Corporate America, I have found there is a huge gap between leaders and employees. We are not in tune with our own emotions, let alone the emotions of others, and when left unchecked, our emotions can lead to some really unfortunate outcomes.

Have you ever been angry and said or done something that you regretted later? I do it on a regular basis. Whether it's yelling at my kids, cursing, or insulting my partner out of frustration, it is evident that my emotions have taken over and run wild.

DEI conversations by nature are emotional. They're about how people feel and how people perceive situations. They're messy and paradoxical. They invite emotion to run freely, which can be a really good thing but also a really harmful thing, when not managed properly.

Code words can be a useful tool for allyship. They can be helpful by interrupting our path to irrational and emotional behavior. They provide us with a momentary pause, right before we say or do something we might regret, to turn on our rational brain for just a second and think about the impact our reaction might have. Considering the potential negative impact that our words or actions might carry can save us from making big mistakes.

I like code words as an allyship tool. As I write this, in my own household we're using the word "gorgonzola." I've worked with leaders over the years who use everything from a nose twitch to the word "yellow." It's really helpful to have language prepared when we're in emotional turmoil. It helps our brains think a little bit more rationally instead of emotionally.

How do they work at home? The idea is to have everyone in your family or group brainstorm words together. There needs to be a common understanding that if someone is expressing a lot of unhelpful emotion, then anyone involved can say the code word. It invites self-awareness into a potentially volatile emotional situation, as well as accountability. Essentially, it's calling someone in, as we further explore in Chapter Eight. The fact that you've agreed to the word ahead of time helps you to settle the emotion and not feel as defensive as you might normally feel.

I was leading a training session recently and a participant was surprised to hear that thirty-one percent of Gen Z identifies as LGBTQ+. Instead of saying they were surprised, though, they said, "I think that's too much."

It was the perception of "too much" that was the problem. The emotion that was expressed across everyone else's faces was obvious. This was a situation where if we had had a code word, we could have easily called that person in and helped them understand the impact of their words. Instead, I had to stop the conversation, educate the person, and disrupt the training for everyone else. Not managing emotions wastes everyone's time.

Neuroscience 101

It helps to have a basic understanding of how the brain works as an ally. The brain has a huge impact on our behavior, emotions, and how we show up in the world. There are three main parts of the brain—the neocortex, the limbic system, and the amygdala. The neocortex is the rational part of the brain right behind the forehead. It's the newest part of the brain and the least utilized. It's responsible for rational thought, data processing, and complex problem-solving.

As humans have evolved over time, the need to use our neocortex has increased significantly. Because most of our human survival was spent hunting and gathering, our limbic system has been the most active part of our brain. It is responsible for our emotions and making quick decisions (or gut instinct) to keep us alive.

In our primal days, when we might have been hunted by a saber-tooth tiger, our fight-or-flight response was essential to our survival. When our amygdala fires up, we become aware that we are in danger and we need to make a quick decision on whether to run or to fight the potential predator. Fast forward to today and our brain confuses innocent things as perceived predators.

Today's emotional triggers could be an email you got from someone, someone pushing back on your ideas, or someone criticizing your work. Not exactly a saber-tooth tiger, but our brains are still wired to protect ourselves and make snap decisions based on our survival. That email or piece of feedback isn't going to kill you, yet your brain reacts very similarly to how it would with a predator.

When my daughter was three, we used to go to the zoo frequently. The rule was if she was well behaved at the zoo and didn't throw a fit when we left, she would get a slushy. On one beautiful, well-behaved day, we were driving home in the car and she decided to take the lid off (foreshadowing is intentional, parents).

We arrived back at home, and as I was unpacking the car, she took her slushy inside and went to sit on the couch to finish it. As you may have guessed, the slushy spilled everywhere. When I entered my living room, all I saw was orange—everywhere! The couch was orange, she was covered in orange, there was orange on the carpet. I felt my muscles clench. My fists balled up, my eyebrows furrowed, and my jaw tightened.

She took one look at me and said, "Mama, you're angry." As a three-year-old, she could recognize the emotions from my body language. I remember telling myself I was being emotionally hijacked and that I wasn't thinking clearly. I took a deep breath, unclenched my fists, and looked at my three-year-old. I said, "Go to the bathroom, please," and then continued to take deep breaths and ask myself, *What do I need to do to feel a little bit better?*

After a few moments, the answer was clear. I needed to get rid of the orange on the couch. I took off the couch cushions, took them outside, and sprayed them off. I then cleaned up the carpet before going to the bathroom and opening the door to let her know she could come out now. She took one look at me and said, "Mama, you're happy now." If a three-year-old can pick up on emotions, we all can.

Within a few minutes, my range of emotions was very obvious to her. I'm not proud of how I reacted that day, as I probably scared my daughter with my emotional reaction. As an ally, if we can read an emotionally charged situation, we can find ways to calm down. Yelling or matching another person's emotions usually makes things worse. Had I not taken those few moments to breathe, been mindful of my body language, I fear I would have said or done something I would have seriously regretted. We all have moments like that; they are what make us human.

Emotions can be deeply connected to the subject of diversity. Sometimes, even mentioning diversity and inclusion can trigger people. It takes them to an emotional place in their brain where they're not able to rationally speak clearly. The words "racism," "sexism," and "homophobia" often have even more polarizing effects on folks.

I can recall a time that I was at a party with my friends and someone casually brought up that they wanted to debate climate change. I perked up. I was so interested. I asked, "Would it be okay if we discussed the intersections of racism with climate change?" The room got quiet, and people found excuses to leave. I found myself alone with the willing debater of climate change, ready to learn about the intersections of racism. Everyone else scattered because they felt uncomfortable. They were afraid they were going to say or do the wrong thing and they didn't understand what we were going to talk about. They forgot to be curious.

Not everyone wants to be an ally.

One of the things that can help us uncover our emotional triggers is a triggers exercise. To do the exercise, think about what happens before you feel emotionally hijacked, the moment before your amygdala (fight-or-flight) takes over and you can't think clearly, just like I couldn't in the orange slushy debacle. What happens right before that moment? What triggers you or what has triggered you in the past? For me it's a mess, someone not making a decision, lack of empathy or inclusion, or someone over-explaining something to me that I already know (because I have studied the subject at length) instead of being curious to learn something from me.

Everyone has triggers. If you're not aware of your triggers, they will most certainly manage you. I recommend that you list three to five triggers and then think about what a positive response would look like in that moment instead of losing control of your rational thought. Then brainstorm positive responses for those triggers. This is really helpful when discussing DEI, because if someone were to say something potentially harmful or microaggress someone in your presence, you might be tempted to become emotional with them. Instead, pause, breathe, or move your body to work off the emotional energy. Then, come back to that conversation. Rarely do emotional conversations achieve positive results for inclusion.

My daughter recently learned about triggers in her second-grade class. One night, in the heat of frustration about her doing her chores, she said to me, "I think I know what your triggers are. You don't like it when I don't do my chores." To which I replied, "Yes, I don't like it when people don't do what they're supposed to do."

Our children can easily pick up on our triggers and often can see them more clearly than we can in the moment. Knowing your triggers can help set and manage expectations of others around you.

It is helpful to have language to describe our emotions. If we don't know how to label our triggers and communicate our emotions when we're feeling them, they can take charge. Think about the people you look up to most in the world. What are their common qualities? I bet one of them is that they are emotionally self-aware. We gravitate towards people who are consistent and secure in their emotions.

Social Emotional Learning

The Collaborative for Academic, Social, and Emotional Learning (CASEL) defines social emotional learning (SEL) as "the process through which all young people and adults acquire and apply the knowledge, skills, and attitudes to develop healthy identities, manage emotions and achieve personal and collective goals, feel and show empathy for others, establish and maintain supportive relationships, and make responsible and caring decisions."

Similar to emotional intelligence, it has the core competencies of self-awareness, self-management, social awareness, relationship skills, and responsible decision-making. As reported by CASEL, SEL has positive outcomes on academic performance, citing an eleven-percentile point gain in achievement for students who practice Social Emotional Learning. However, SEL has become a controversial issue amongst many school systems and board meetings. Similar to misunderstandings about critical race theory, SEL has been used as a propaganda campaign to scare parents.

Lack of awareness is one of the primary problems with DEI. For us to be able to have empathetic, vulnerable conversations about differences, we must know how to process our emotions. This doesn't have to be complicated. While emotions might feel very complex, having a simple guide to describe your emotions with young people (all people for that matter) is helpful.

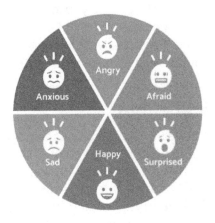

The SEL color wheel breaks our emotions down into six basic categories: red for angry, orange for afraid, yellow for surprised, green for happy, blue for sad, and purple for anxious. Most people, when asked to brainstorm emotions, tend to keep them very basic and will generally cite sad, happy, or mad. The color wheel gives kids language for more complex emotions and a shortcut, similar to a code word, to explain to them.

When talking about emotions, it's important to understand that not all emotions are positive. On the color wheel there's a wide range of emotions. Yet more often when someone shares something hard or painful with us, like a DEI conflict, we often react wanting to make it better with a positive wrapper (or Band-Aid) around their sad or painful story.

"Toxic positivity is forced, false positivity. It may sound innocuous on the surface, but when you share something difficult with someone and they insist that you turn it into a positive, what they're really saying is, `My comfort is more important than your reality'." Susan David

When people in our personal lives express emotions, especially young people, it's important to meet them where they're at. It's okay for them to feel that way. It's okay for them to find a place to process their emotion and come back to the conversation when they're ready. It's okay for them to set boundaries around their emotions and to tell people if they're not being treated according to their boundaries.

One of my friends has a special mat at her house and it has a curtain around it. When her children are expressing difficult emotions, they know to go to the mat and close the curtain and that that's a safe place for them to process their emotions, a place where no one will intervene until they are ready. It's another tool that makes processing emotions in difficult situations easier. Creating tools when we're calm and rational can be helpful to use in situations where it's hard to think clearly because we're emotional.

Psychological safety is a shared belief held by members of a team that others on the team will not embarrass, reject, or punish you for speaking up.

I liken psychological safety to feeling safe when saying and doing hard things. There's not going to be an adverse reaction, punishment, or retribution for speaking up and saying something unpopular. As allies, this has to be the case to have productive conversations about the challenges of diversity. If we don't feel safe bringing up hard things like racism, sexism, and homophobia, then we're never going to get to the real issues that are holding people back.

Allies do hard things.

A friend of mine, Linda, is Black. She shared a story with me years ago that stuck with me. She lives in a predominantly White neighborhood. She has a dog and walks him regularly there. She shared with me that on more than one occasion, she has been stopped by people in her own neighborhood and asked if she is the dog walker. That's just not something that has happened to me as a White woman. I can't imagine being in my own neighborhood and not feeling like I belong, likely because of my skin color.

If you're thinking this isn't a big deal, imagine how you would respond if you were Linda. If you respond emotionally, then you would fit the stereotype of an "angry Black woman." It takes energy to keep your cool when you are microaggressed, and people of color, women, LGBTQ+ folks, and those with disabilities have to process their emotional responses a lot more than the majority group.

So, what do we do as allies? Here is something I try to do in my predominantly White neighborhood. I go for walks every day and when I see people of different races, ethnicities, or different types of families, I intentionally try to help them feel welcome. I genuinely greet them and say "hello" in a pleasant way. Not that I wouldn't do that with somebody who looks like me, but I know that person already probably feels welcome, so they don't need that extra smile and effort as much as somebody else who looks different might appreciate it. Linda's story helped me understand that I have a role in helping everyone feel welcome in all places.

My friend Tamyra is Black and always attends my daughter's birthday parties. She is typically one of the few people of color at the party. When she walks in, I try my best to greet her and hug her to show her how welcome she is. She has shared with me that she is used to being the only Black person in a lot of places. I don't want to be a savior, as my behavior isn't to save Tamyra. She's very strong and capable and doesn't need me to do anything special for her. My extra attention to her is more to signal to others that she belongs. That's the fine balance of allyship. It never looks and feels perfect. It is awkward and brave.

Compassion Fatigue

According to the Pew Research Center, seventy-five percent of adults believe it is "very or somewhat important" for companies and organizations to promote diversity. This means that twenty-five percent of people do not think DEI is important. Not everyone is an ally.

Don't waste time on those who don't want to get it. DEI work is emotionally exhausting, and you have to protect your energy. It can be difficult to unlearn and relearn things and hear stories about the adversity of diversity (though still not comparable to the trauma of living with discrimination and adversity). Allies realize that DEI is a long game. Most of the population believes DEI is important and wants to understand it, but they don't get it yet, meaning that they need tools and education. I call this the "magic middle." Sometimes my clients call this the "frozen middle."

How do we help reach the magic middle while protecting our own energy?

Critical mass theory indicates that it takes thirty percent of a population to be represented for things to start shifting. This has been used often with women on boards. Once there's thirty percent representation of women on boards, we start to see positive change. The same goes for allies. Once we can reach thirty percent of the population and get them on board with DEI, we will arrive at the tipping point. We are very close to that number. So, if you can influence people around you to join the conversation and to better understand DEI by reading some books or listening to some podcasts, we could reach that tipping point in our lifetimes.

If you want to be a part of the tipping point, set goals for yourself to practice allyship every day. It could be something as subtle as having a conversation with somebody who's different than you, advocating for someone different than you, or learning more about the ever-evolving topic of DEI. Pick something and keep going. Commit to being on the ally journey long-term.

A client of mine was asked by her DEI leader at work why she cared about DEI. She was unsure what to say but leaned into her vulnerability and shared her personal story. She's married to a Black man and is White; her children are mixed-race. She has a five-year-old boy, and she knows she needs to have a conversation with him soon about how people might perceive him, how he might have to act around police to stay safe, and how he might need to dress to make others not feel intimidated. None of this is fair for them, but it is the reality. She anticipates the day when her boy will ask questions like, "If you knew about this, Mom, why didn't you do anything about it?"

What are you willing to do about it?

To protect yourself against compassion fatigue, channel that boy's question. If you're on the journey and you're continuing to educate yourself and others around you, modeling positive ally behavior, you can say you're doing something about it. If you stay silent and come into the conversation only when it's popular, you can't answer that question confidently. On hard days, when people challenge me or it feels like nothing's getting better or the change is stagnant, I think about this next generation of little allies. They simply deserve better. Me giving up because it's hard isn't an option. That would be the ultimate misuse of my privilege to not have to keep doing the hard work.

Allies practice emotional agility. Each chapter has a short assessment to better understand where you are and where you want to be as an ally. Consider these assessment results before moving forward with another ally skill set.

Assessment:

- ☐ I understand the neuroscience of emotions.
- ☐ I am aware of my emotions.
- ☐ I read and respond appropriately to the emotions of others.
- ☐ I support social emotional learning.
- ☐ I manage my emotional triggers.
- ☐ I find safe places to process my emotions.
- ☐ I ensure the psychological safety of others around me.
- ☐ I believe most people want to be better allies for diversity.
- ☐ I commit to helping others learn to be better allies.
- ☐ I understand the role emotions play in diversity.

Emotions Reader Activity

Visualization Exercise

One of the ways you can show up as an ally in all aspects of your life is to start to visualize yourself doing just that. The more we visualize ourselves doing something, the more we can start to implement the small habits that turn into a lifestyle.

1. Grab a journal or device for you to write down your thoughts.
2. Visualize yourself leading like an ally in all aspects of your life. It might help to write down the major areas of your life, such as work, home, friendships, etc.
3. Write down everything that comes to mind without worrying about what you are saying or how you are saying it. Keep it your most honest thoughts.
4. How could you start implementing small actions or habits to make your vision a reality? Write down some thoughts for each area of your life.

Emotions Group or Family Activity

Materials:

-Emotions color wheel (To find this, do a Google search for 'emotions color wheel.' There will be a lot of options so just select the one that works best for you!)

Directions:
-Pull out the emotions color wheel with your group.
-Say: "What are some emotions that you feel? When do you normally feel those emotions?"
-Look at the emotions color wheel together.
- Point to a word and say: "What does this emotion feel like? What does it look like? Have you experienced this? When? What do you do when you feel that way? What can you do more or less of in those situations?"
-Now that you have talked about emotions and the emotions wheel, use it in real time with your group members when they're experiencing big emotions. Try this conversation:
-Reassure and validate. It might sound something like, "Everyone experiences all kinds of emotions—kids and adults. Emotions aren't a bad thing. Sometimes our emotions can make us act in a way that we didn't intend, but that's why it's important to talk about them in a safe space. We always want to learn from our emotions."
-"Can you point to which emotion you were feeling when it happened?"
-"What were you thinking when it happened?"
-"What did you do? Is that what you meant to do?"
-"How would you handle it differently next time?"

-You may want to model processing emotions by telling your group members about an event that happened to you that day and how you were feeling based on the emotions wheel.

CHAPTER SIX: COURAGE

Active allyship at home necessitates courage. It's not enough to read books like this, listen to podcasts, or wait for someone to tell you what to do to show up as an ally. You are the only one who can decide the kind of ally you want to be. That could be a mentor, a friend, a supporter, an advocate, a listener, an inclusive educator, or a caregiver. Allyship is personal.

DEI starts with "U."

Following the resurgence of the Black Lives Matter and long overdue racial justice movement in 2020, there were a lot of well-intentioned White people who entered the conversation. They proclaimed themselves to be allies. They showed up at protests and posted pictures on social media. Many of those well-intentioned folks did not stay in the conversation. They returned to their normal lives once it was no longer in the news cycle and popular to post about.

This behavior is extremely harmful to people of color and those most marginalized in our culture. It feels like people are taking advantage of the situation when it benefits them and are not willing to stay with the work when things get tough. That's not what allyship is. It's not a self-proclamation. It is a daily intentional practice. Allyship is helping people different from you. Sometimes it requires pain, personal loss, and shifting of privilege.

In fact, according to the Pew Research Center, at the peak of Black Lives Matter in the summer of 2020, social acceptance of the movement was at sixty-seven percent. Fast forward a year to 2021, and social acceptance declined to fifty-five percent. Why the decline? A lot of well-intentioned allies who wanted to be supportive quickly realized this is hard work. Rolling up your sleeves and actively participating in hard conversations can be exhausting when you are not used to it. Unlearning and relearning is hard on our brains. It is easier to keep things the same. As the old saying goes, "if it isn't broken, don't fix it."

The system is broken.

Active allyship is about addressing systemic change. It addresses the various systems that we have set up as a society—education, housing, voting, policing, healthcare—that keep the majority group at an advantage and the underrepresented groups at a disadvantage. Allies use their voices for positive change. They don't accept excuses like, "Those people don't work as hard" or "They don't want it for themselves." They address these myths of meritocracy and debunk them in the moment.

Allies are familiar with calling people into conversations. They see problematic situations as opportunities to reshape perceptions and reach a broader understanding as a group. They don't hide when things get tough. They realize their silence Is compliance.

The Ladder of Inference

One of the tools we love in the inclusive leadership world with our corporate clients is the ladder of inference, first coined by Chris Argyris and Peter Senge in *The Fifth Discipline: The Art and Practice of the Learning Organization.*

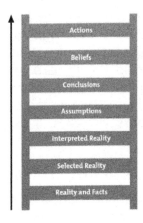

The idea is, as human beings, we make snap decisions very regularly. As discussed in earlier chapters, our brains like comfortable, routine decisions and like to save our mental capacity for hard decisions. We often make decisions based on our beliefs. Our beliefs are informed by our childhoods, our experiences, and who we surround ourselves by on a daily basis.

We like to stay at the top of the ladder. We rarely work our way down the ladder to explore all of the data available to us. Even when we work our way all the way down and examine the full reality and facts available, we often select the version of the facts that we like the most. This is called confirmation bias. We actively look for information that supports what we already believe to be true. This results in our interpreted reality of the situation, informing our assumptions and the conclusions that are used to cement our beliefs and justify our actions.

Let's practice using an example. Say you're in a difficult conversation about DEI with someone. A disagreement arises over a text exchange. Both of you point to the same string of text messages as evidence supporting your beliefs and actions, but neither one of you have worked your way down the ladder to all the available information and context that informed those text messages.

No one thought about prior conversations and how they impact this text string. No one thought to ask clarifying questions rather than draw conclusions. And again, no one thought to double-check their assumptions with actual facts and information.

The majority of conflicts about DEI exist because we're unwilling to work ourselves down the ladder and see the situation objectively. Our emotional brains don't like to spend that type of mental energy on conflicts. Only by taking the time to work our way down the ladder can we actually get to the root cause. Spending an hour having a conversation about the real root of the conflict, as friends, could save dozens of angry text strings over time.

Remember to flip the script in a conflict situation by asking yourself these questions: What's the other person's perspective? How might they come up with a different conclusion? What facts do I have available to make a well-informed decision? What if this person had positive intentions? What would that look like?

Allies assume positive intent.

Positive intention is a double-edged sword. On one hand, believing people are coming from a good place helps you be more empathetic as an ally. It helps you find the courage to work your way down the ladder. On the other hand, letting people justify harmful actions with positive intention can create more harm than good. Accountability, layered with positive intention, is key.

A few years ago, I was at a sporting event with friends. We were having a great time until one of my friends made a gesture with his arm and said, "I am going to tomahawk you." At that moment, I positioned my body aggressively and said, "You can't say that. You're racist."

I reacted. I didn't take time to respond or work my way down the ladder. I didn't practice positive intent. I shamed my friend in front of our group of friends. Of course, what he said was wrong—he is White, and it is culturally insensitive to talk about Native American cultural traditions without understanding their origins or meanings—but calling him out, in this case, as a racist, was unhelpful and confrontational.

I'm not proud of what I did that day. I wish I could say that that event shifted things for my friend, or we had a good conversation and found a way to work down the ladder later, but we didn't. It is very difficult to have conversations with him now about diversity, and a lot of that is because I didn't stay open that day.

I use a much softer approach when I find myself in these situations with my White male friends. I do not tiptoe, but instead, meet them where they're at. If they say a potentially harmful term or express a microaggression, for instance, I simply shake my head and say, "We don't say that anymore" or "That's not okay." What I learned is that outing somebody in front of a group or calling them racist, sexist, or homophobic in front of people is going to lead to more negative outcomes than positive ones.

Courageous conversations are generally better one-on-one (unless you have a high degree of trust as a group). I personally like to pull somebody aside or ask for time later and say, "Can we unpack what happened there?" I often use the Situation-Behavior-Impact (SBI) model in my corporate work. In a courageous conversation at home, you can easily paint the picture of the situation with the who, what, where, and when, then talk about specific behaviors—the actual things someone said or did, with the potential harmful impacts to the group as a result of their behavior.

Most people prefer feedback rather than people talking about them behind their backs. How we frame that feedback matters. Be sure to use "I" statements instead of "you" statements. Be specific to actual behavior and not perceptions, asking open-ended questions to explore what you don't know, and work down the ladder.

Address Microaggressions

Microaggressions are small and harmful statements most people have said, heard, or participated in. They happen at a much higher frequency to women, people of color, those in the LGBTQ+ community, and those with disabilities.

Here are some common microaggressions:

- Where are you *really* from?
- Stop being bossy (to a woman).
- What are you?
- Let me explain that to you (or, you would not understand).
- You don't act like a normal (BIPOC, woman, disability, LGBTQ+ person).
- I don't see you as a (BIPOC, woman, disability, LGBTQ+).
- You don't speak (language)?
- People think it's weird I listen to (music).
- You smell like (ethnic food).
- Can I touch your hair?
- Is that a (BIPOC, woman, disability, LGPTQ+) culture thing?

Other common microaggressions are interruptions, taking credit for someone else's idea, and "splaining" to someone else. There are many flavors of "splaining"—

mansplaining, whitesplaining, straightsplaining, non-disabled explaining. "Splaining" is when the majority group explains what it's like to be someone from an underrepresented group when they don't have the context of the lived experiences. Allies always follow the lead of people different from them. They never assume they know what it's like to be the other person or make broad assumptions based on their limited view.

You might be thinking to yourself, *People actually say these things out loud?* Compare notes with somebody different than you. You'd be surprised that these experiences are extremely common and frequent for people with diverse backgrounds. They still happen today and certainly aren't issues of the past.

The toll that microaggressions take is cumulative. One or two are easier to shrug off than three or four, but after five and up, people hit a tipping point. This is known as weathering. Weathering is the aggregated impact of racism, from the systemic to interpersonal, leading to premature biological aging and worse health outcomes for Black people.

When we stand by and let microaggressions happen, we are bystanders. By definition, if you are not speaking up when bad things happen, you are contributing to the problem. Allies are not bystanders; they're upstanders, meaning they don't stand by when they witness non-inclusive things. If someone says or does something that's not inclusive or microaggresses someone when they are present, allies take action.

Upstanders ask themselves these questions:

- What if I say nothing?
- Am I okay with this happening again?
- What if my child/friend did this?

By reflecting on these questions, you will deepen your thinking and move beyond a primal emotional reaction to a more well-thought-out response. You can choose your words more carefully and practice empathy towards the person who needs help understanding why their behavior was harmful. More importantly, it signals to the people around witnessing the behavior that this is not okay, and it creates safety for the person who's being microaggressed. They will feel as though someone has their back.

Ally Watch-Outs

Many well-intentioned allies-in-training make mistakes. We call it the bumble and stumble of allyship. By definition, learning requires us to make mistakes. You don't know what you don't know yet. Be kind to yourself, give yourself space and grace as you're learning, and practice good self-care to maintain your energy.

Common early allyship mistakes include:

- Saviorism (saving the day for the other person).
- Making excuses for bad behavior (rather than holding the person accountable).
- Defending or denying your own bad behavior (rather than apologizing).
- Trying too hard (not everything is about DEI).
- Participating in allyship only when it is in the spotlight (following the news cycle).

According to the McKinsey 2021 Women in the Workplace report, seventy-seven percent of people consider themselves to be allies at work. Very few of these people advocate (twenty-one percent), confront discrimination (thirty-nine percent), mentor or sponsor (ten percent), or take real action to show they are allies at work. While this data is from the workplace, allyship has similar correlations at home. People often think they're doing more than they really are. Everyone wants to think they are a good person, and no one wants to believe that they are intentionally harming someone else.

A colleague of mine recently shared his allyship story with me. He works in an industry that is extremely White, non-disabled, straight male-dominated (nearly all industries are). In fact, his entire team is White, straight, non-disabled males, including himself. When I asked him what shifted for him to want to focus on diversity, he responded that he feels his lifelong calling is to bring more people into the industry that he's loved since he was a child. He wants to see his own children better reflected and those who are different reflected in the industry he loves. He sees DEI as additive. To bring more people into his industry benefits his business, as well as his own personal passion to share what he loves with others. When the time comes to retire, he wants to leave the industry more inclusive than how he found it.

Ally visions help us find courage when things get hard. A client of mine candidly shared a few years ago that he attended an industry conference where a Black man presented a talk about anti-racism. The speaker advocated that the systems need positive change. My client was early in his ally journey at the time and was really caught off-guard by the presentation. He was even offended. He recalls feeling emotionally defensive and felt like he was accused of being a part of the problem just because he was White.

Today, he actively understands his role in maintaining the systems that keep certain people down. He's further along on his ally journey because he's acknowledged that, although he is indeed part of the problem, he can choose to be part of the solution. He actively looks for ways to engage people of color, women, those with disabilities, and LGBTQ+ folks in a very White, straight, male-dominated industry. He doesn't do it for the glory; he does it because he understands he has an obligation to leverage his privilege for good. Although his journey began with denial, it has flourished into awareness and advocacy.

At the beginning of an ally journey, it is not uncommon for people to be unwilling to accept their role in the systems that they didn't personally create. It's a very natural reaction to deny things that are different than you believe them to be. It's easier to say, "I didn't create these systems," or "I'm a good person." That's not the point. Being an ally is accepting that you benefit from these systems, and you can participate in changing them. It's the paradox of accepting "I'm a good person and I also make mistakes."

My nephew is a White, straight, cisgender, non-disabled male. He was born and raised in a small rural Midwest area that has a problematic racial past and strong perceptions of racism still today. He's incredibly bright and hard-working and didn't have a ton of resources growing up. He did the best he could with what he had. Similar to the myth of meritocracy, my nephew surpassed people's expectations of him. He was valedictorian of his high school class, the second student ever from his high school to go to an Ivy League college, and he is rocking a 4.0 as a sophomore there, as I write this book.

He and I have had several candid conversations about DEI. One Thanksgiving, he openly acknowledged his privilege without any prompting. I simply responded, "How did you realize you had it?" He said he's observed other people not be taken as seriously or not given the same chances as him, even though his life was not easy. He worked very hard to get to where he is at, and he wants to share his privilege with others. He sees it as a chance to help others who are different from him. Privilege is not a zero-sum game. Admitting you have privilege does not mean that you did not work hard. It just means you have a duty to help others with what you have.

White men are not the problem with DEI. They are the solution.

I am married to a White man, my nephew is a White man, and many of my friends and clients are White men. They are not the enemy. We have to bring White men into the conversation about DEI to move it forward. Our systems are controlled by White men, they created the systems, and we need them to participate in helping change the systems.

It's not fair to expect those most marginalized to fix problems they didn't create.

Having the courage to hold people accountable for their actions is part of the ally journey. Part of allyship is coming to terms with our own limitations, owning them vs. running from them, and inspiring others to do the same. Each chapter has a short assessment to better understand where you are and where you want to be as an ally. Consider these assessment results before moving forward with another ally skill set.

Assessment:

- ☐ I understand the ladder of inference.
- ☐ I attempt to work down the ladder of inference.
- ☐ I am aware of my assumptions.
- ☐ I see conflict as an opportunity to learn.
- ☐ I am an upstander.
- ☐ When I see something, I say something.
- ☐ I am aware of microaggressions I have a tendency to commit.
- ☐ I address my microaggressions with humility.
- ☐ I point out the microaggressions of others.
- ☐ I see mistakes as a part of the ally journey.

Courage Reader Activity

Your Implicit Biases

When we come into contact with confusing, unclear, or unfamiliar information, we try to make sense of it based on what we already know. This is how implicit bias happens. When we come into contact with something new, different, or confusing, we quickly make unconscious associations in our minds, even when we don't mean to.

For this exercise, see how your brain makes sense of the given confusing information. Try to read the sentences below:

If you can raed tihs it is bceuase our mndis hvae laenred how to put tgoehter new or ucnlaer ifnmoramtoin in a way taht is esay to mkae snsee of bsaed on the cnotxet gvien. Our mndis are albe to do tihs wtihuot our concsuios cnrotol.

Now read this version:

If you can read this it is because our minds have learned how to put together new or unclear information in a way that is easy to make sense of based on the context given. Our minds are able to do this without our conscious control.

This exercise was adapted from: The Kirwan Institute
Reflect:

When you come into contact with something or someone new or different, what are you thinking? Pay attention to your thoughts this week that may reveal implicit bias.

Courage Group or Family Activity

Materials:
-No materials needed for this exercise, unless you would like to have physical items or pictures to help group members see what you are talking about

Directions:
1. Have a discussion with your group about microaggressions. Present the following scenarios to the group and talk about what they would do if they were in this situation. Here are some questions to ask:
a. What do you think about this situation?
b. Is it wrong to do/say what they did? Why or why not?
c. What would you do if you saw this happen?
2. Scenario 1: A White student in your class says to a Black student: "You're smarter than the other Black kids in this class."
3. Scenario 2: A boy says to a girl: "You can't play with that toy. It's for boys."
4. Scenario 3: Your friend says to a stranger in a wheelchair: "What happened to your leg?"
5. Scenario 4: A group of White kids says to a new kid who is Mexican: "You can't sit with us. You don't belong."
6. Scenario 5: A White girl says to a Black girl: "Can I touch your hair?"

CHAPTER SEVEN: COACHING

Coaching may feel like a term that is only used in sports arenas or professional settings, but coaching can have a profound impact on our personal lives as well. In this chapter we will explore various coaching skills and how you can apply them in your personal life as an ally.

The main objective of a coach is to create space for others to learn and grow. As humans, our most primal needs are to feel seen, heard, and like we belong. When someone creates that space for us, it unlocks our humanity. Only then can we have the confidence to solve problems we didn't think we'd be able to solve and be vulnerable about our shortcomings and challenges with others.

Coaches don't judge people for what they share; they protect the privacy of others and maintain confidentiality. They simply sit back, listen, and ask questions to promote self-discovery. While sports coaches motivate, instruct, and develop the skills of their teams, coaching an ally is different. It is more about helping someone motivate themselves, not giving them the answers, and instead helping them solve their own problems. This is a more sustainable approach as an ally. If we constantly save the day for people, give them advice, or tell them what to do, then they only learn to rely on us for solutions. It is overwhelming to feel like you have to constantly solve other people's problems.

Allies sit with others in their pain.

Refrain from giving advice to those you want to be an ally for, and instead sit with someone in their pain. When we sit with someone and experience their problems and challenges with them, they feel less alone. Not being included can feel isolating, especially to someone who feels like they're being marginalized. Rarely do people want someone to wave a magic wand for them and save the day. They want to be heard, to feel like you understand their problem and empathize with their situation.

As humans, we are wired to solve problems quickly. In previous chapters we have covered the neuroscience of our brains and our tendency to make snap decisions. We don't like to experience problems that we don't know how to solve. This is why our brains tend to jump to conclusions instead of working down the ladder of inference to examine all of the information. Our brain doesn't want us to feel bad, so we like to put Band-Aids on gigantic wounds.

When allies see someone hurting, they dig deeper instead of glossing over.

Allies resist the urge to make it better for the other person by staying curious to listen to learn. They immerse themselves in the pain; they don't avoid the pain. They see pain as a vehicle to dig deeper into the root cause. Through this skill, coaching can bring more allies into the DEI conversation.

Listening

There's a lot of content out there about the importance of active listening. Most people think they are better listeners than they actually are. In fact, even when we are actively listening, we usually only hear about fifty percent of what the other person is actually saying. We listen for things we understand, have experienced ourselves, or jump to quick solutions when others are speaking. We rarely clear our minds of thought and listen.

I have an ally who is an incredible listener. We've been friends for several years, but early on in our relationship I took advantage of her profound listening skills. When we would go out for breakfast or go for a walk, I would dump all my problems on her, and being the kind of person she was, she let me vent. She rarely tried to problem-solve. She would just nod her head as she was listening and say, "I get it," or "That would suck," or "I have no idea what that feels like." She gave me the space to think through my problems and rarely offered advice. At the end of our conversations, I would have ideas about what to do, but not ideas that she'd given me. Ideas that she led me to by giving me the space to think out loud with her and come up with on my own.

Today, we still enjoy our walks together, but now we take turns sharing our successes and challenges. I have more awareness of how much I'm listening vs. speaking in our conversations. She has a lot going on in her life now and it's my turn to listen to her. I rarely have the solutions to her problems because I don't know what it's like to be her, but as an ally, my goal is to acknowledge her pain, listen to understand, and acknowledge the successes she's had.

I have another friend, whom I have known since childhood and who knows me better than anyone on the planet. She and her family immigrated to the US when she was ten years old. Growing up, it was fun to spend time with her family, hear different words, observe different traditions, and gain exposure to another culture. Because she knows me so well, it's really easy for her to listen to my problems and make suggestions about what I should do. I love that she's a natural problem-solver, wants to be helpful, and cares deeply about me. She is my biggest advocate when something non-inclusive happens in my life. I know she does not want to see me in pain.

After a few times of really wanting to just vent to her and not have her solve my problems, I had to tell her, "This is a time when I need you to listen, not problem-solve."

It felt very difficult to be so direct, but she really appreciated me giving her that feedback and it's helped us have more open conversations. That's what allies do. They are clear up front with their expectations and talk about hard things. They know that listening is the best tool in their tool kit.

Allies listen to learn.

So, if you want to be a better ally to people different than you, start with listening—active listening, meaning that you are focused intently on what the other person is saying, not what you think or what you would do. You suspend judgment and focus one hundred percent of your energy on learning more about what the person is sharing with you. Instead of filling in with an assumption when you don't know something, you instead choose to ask a question.

In addition to listening, playbacks are another key skill for coaching. Playbacks can be very effective. In fact, research has shown that playing back someone's exact words signals to the other person that they have been heard and presents the opportunity to clear up any misconceptions. They also give you, and the person you are talking with, the time to process what has been said. Studies have shown that people feel awkward with silence around second two, but often we need at least seven seconds to think more deeply about our responses. I call this the seven second rule. As allies, if we give someone seven seconds, while it might feel awkward in the moment, there is usually something very beautiful, candid, and deep in their response. Our brains need time to process.

When I'm struggling with active listening, during the seven seconds, I will recite a mantra in my head that helps me focus on listening. For instance, I repeat, *It will come,* or I imagine a relaxing nature scene to take my mind off of the awkward silence. When practicing this with clients, I'll often reach for my drink and pause to take a long sip of water or purposely look around the room and not stare intently at them to give them the space to think. People need space to think about hard things like DEI.

If DEI was an easy problem to solve, we would have solved it already.

Asking Open Questions

When I first started my DEI consulting business, I went through a Master Coach Certification program. One of the tools I was taught was the "what do you want" exercise. Essentially, it's a repetitive exercise in asking the question "what do you want" across all facets of your life— financial, spiritual, health, wellness, career, family, relationships, etc.

As a professional coach I often use this tool when I begin working with a client one-on-one to map out their priorities and goals. This also works well in casual allyship conversations. If you want to understand someone who's different from you, figure out what matters to them the most. For some people it's family, for others it's career, and for some it's their health. Those priorities change throughout the course of our lives. If you don't understand what motivates someone or what their priorities are, it's difficult to be with them as an ally.

Just like active listening, asking open-ended questions is a key skill for coaching as an ally. Even when I do exercises with people where I tell them they can only ask open-ended questions, they still default to closed-ended questions. Our brains are wired for certainty, and we do not like asking questions that we, ourselves, don't know the answers to.

Allies ask questions they do not know the answers to.

When asking open-ended questions, there are two words that help significantly—*what* and *how*. They make it very difficult to ask a question that's closed-ended. Simply replacing any closed question that begins with *do, could, should, would,* or *are* with *what* or *how* completely changes the tone of a conversation. *What* or *how* require more elaborate responses, rather than the yes or no answers that are likely prompted by *do, could, should, would,* or *are.*

Let's go through some examples of how we might flip closed-ended questions and open-ended questions as allies. For example:

- Do you have any questions? Replace with: What questions do you have?
- Do you think you should do this? Replace with: What do you think?
- Are you going to do this? Replace with: What are you going to do?
- Why do you think that? Replace with: How did you get there?
- Would you be open to...? Replace with: How do you feel about...?

Notice the subtle shift and think about how you would answer the questions on the left versus the right. It's likely you would answer a closed-ended question with a yes, no, or short, simple response. However, with a *what* or *how* question, it's more likely that you would dig deeper and answer the question with more information.

As allies, information is our friend, and the more we know, the more we can help someone. If we think that we know the answer and then ask closed-ended questions, we confirm our assumptions and hear only what we already believe to be true.

Another useful tool that I learned from my coaching certification is the GROW framework, the simple acronym that stands for goal, reality, options, and will. I think of it as a conversation map. It's not a script; it's questions I can utilize, as needed, without interrupting the natural flow of a conversation.

Coaching conversations are not interviews. Allies are not looking to check boxes. We ask questions that are relevant to the situation and designed to help others move from point A to point B. For someone who is experiencing pain with DEI, it can be hard to open up, but by having this framework to prepare yourself for a hard conversation, you are more likely to successfully and confidently navigate it.

I faced my own challenges early on when I was getting my coaching certification. I was excited to try my newly learned skill on everyone in my life, and I was trying too hard. People felt like I was prying and asking intrusive questions even though I was coming from a good place. Don't make my same mistake. Let the conversation flow naturally, and use the GROW framework when you feel stuck. I find it to be an incredibly helpful guide for conversations as an ally.

Here is how the GROW framework works:

- Goal: The intent is to focus on what success looks like and to understand the main point of the conversation. Perhaps it's a specific problem (the gap between a desired state and current state for someone—by definition). One of the most powerful goal questions that you can ask is: What do you want?

- Reality: This is where the pain comes in. Well-intentioned allies may gloss over the pain people are experiencing. Racism, sexism, homophobia, ableism, and ageism are difficult to approach. It's tempting to avoid because we are uncomfortable when others express their pain associated with feeling less than. We have to overcome this in order to sit with people in their pain. Allies should ask questions like: What are your barriers? What are the root causes of the issue? What do you wish was happening that's not?

- Options: This is where we love to spend our time—brainstorming solutions to the problems you have identified. You can easily flip the pain points and turn them into potential solutions. I love using statements like: Let's brainstorm. What are your ideas? Or if someone gets stuck, ask them: If another one of our allies was here, what would they say?

- Will: This is one step that we often overlook. After we've had a robust conversation with someone and helped them map out potential solutions to their problems, it is important to remember commitment. Spend the last few minutes of your conversation asking: What did we decide to do today? What is your next step? What is your timeline? What does support look like? Asking these questions can be great for establishing accountability. Good allies let others know that they have their backs by helping them be accountable.

Allies help others be accountable.

I have an ally who came to me with a challenge she was facing. Her oldest daughter had just come out as bisexual and this news came as a huge surprise to her deeply religious family. Both she and her husband didn't know what to do. As she was sharing her story with me, my mind started spinning with the many tools and resources I know of to support the LGBTQ+ community. As I was listening, I was also trying to map out a plan for her because I cared and I didn't want to see her in pain.

Though, as I listened, I realized she had a lot more answers within than she initially thought. She had bought a book to better understand the situation, she had already had the difficult conversations with her partner who didn't know how to be supportive as well, and she had really listened to her daughter to better understand. She acknowledged her mistakes and made a firm commitment to be a better ally to her daughter. She acknowledged that commitment with, "I want her to feel fully supported by us."

It was only through asking simple open-ended questions like, "Help me understand," "What do you know?" "What don't you understand?" and "What kind of support do you think she needs?" that enabled her to think it through on her own.

Putting on the coaching hat is never easy when we are compelled to jump in and problem-solve. Resist the temptation for instant gratification as an ally. Give people that extra space to listen. While it might feel like a longer conversation, you save time by addressing the real problem and not just the surface level issues.

Self-Discovery

There are a few rules for effective coaching. First, coaching is not advice-giving. Second, the focus should always be forward and not backward (thus different from therapy). Third, we must lose our ego when approaching a conversation. Now, these are all easier to say than to actually do; that is why coaching is often called a practice.

You must practice coaching as an ally. At first, you might find it a little awkward, but over time people will genuinely appreciate being listened to and being given the space to think out loud. Trust builds with repetition and creates a deeper relationship with the people you care about.

Do you remember being a kid and your parents asking you to do something over and over? How did you feel? I remember that I detested cleaning my hamster's cage. My mom would ask repeatedly, and I would procrastinate the monthly cleaning. However, if I decided that the hamster cage was smelly and needed cleaning myself and took the initiative to clean it before my mom asked, the process was much less painful. That's the thing - when people give us advice or tell us what to do, it can be far less motivating. As individuals we are more committed to our own ideas and our decisions. This is the power of self-discovery.

Coaching is also about focusing forward. An ally of mine used to say, "There is a reason the windshield is bigger than the rearview mirror," when we were struggling to move forward in a project.

I love this analogy because we can see much more looking forward than we can by looking back. Coaching is not about dwelling in someone's pain. It's about acknowledging the pain points and guiding them to solutions.

To effectively coach someone different from you, you don't have to be their therapist. Therapy is excellent for deep, personal issues. Coaching is more about helping guide someone forward. It's almost like a shadow beside somebody helping them steer when they don't know how to steer for themselves. They are still in control; you are just helping them stay focused.

Allies don't make it about themselves. They drop their egos and focus solely on the other person. The minute we make the conversation about us, we shift the energy towards us. For instance, if we mention, "That reminds me of the time when that happened to me," or "Here's what I would do in your situation," we teach the person that we're there to problem-solve. The other person will take your cue and not work to solve their problem on their own. Essentially, we are teaching them to rely on us, which might feel good in the short-term but can prove unhelpful in the long-term.

I remember a few years ago when I became certified in Unconscious Bias after a two-day, immersive workshop learning a lot of things that shifted my perspectives significantly. It was painful, but I desperately wanted to share everything I learned with all my friends and family. The problem was they had not gone through the same immersive experience, did not understand a lot of what I was talking about, and weren't that interested.

I remember one of my family members saying, "I don't get it," to me. They went on to deny racism's existence and make some really significant microaggressions about race by questioning if it was still even an issue. Initially, I was floored by the comment. My blood pressure increased, my emotions ran high, and I struggled with self-control. I took a few deep breaths and asked them to go for a walk with me.

We then talked it through while walking outside. I chose to listen first. I asked open-ended questions about their perceptions with genuine curiosity. I asked, "What makes you think that?" "What do you think the real problem is?" "What might be some ways we could be supportive of those problems?" and "What shifted for you as a result of this conversation?"

At the end of the conversation, the person hugged me and said they were thankful that I had listened to them. They were so used to people judging them and not being listened to that they really felt lost in the conversation about race as a White person. They'd learned to not talk about it for fear of saying and doing the wrong thing.

I don't always get it right as an ally. This is a time when coaching worked for me. Sometimes, I forget to use coaching in conversations when emotions take over. We're all allies-in-training. This critical skill will help you navigate tough conversations about DEI.

If we're afraid and not willing to listen, there's no way we can learn to be allies for one another.

We're all allies-in-training. Each chapter has a short assessment to better understand where you are and where you want to be as an ally. Consider these assessment results before moving forward with another ally skill set.

Assessment:

- ☐ I listen to learn.
- ☐ I am an active listener.
- ☐ I know when I speak, I only hear what I already know.
- ☐ I ask open-ended questions.
- ☐ I practice the GROW model.
- ☐ I see the value of self-discovery.
- ☐ I refrain from giving others advice.
- ☐ I do not make conversations about me.
- ☐ I believe in guiding people rather than telling them what to do.
- ☐ I coach others to success.

Coaching Group or Family Activity

Materials:
- Paper
- Writing utensils (You may want to get "fancier" paper/writing utensils if you want to hang this up somewhere later on.)

Directions:

1. Help your group members learn how to speak positive affirmations or a positive mantra over themselves consistently. You will be coming up with one together and finding a creative way to implement it into your/their routine.

2. Start with one person at a time and ask these questions:

   a. "What words would you use to describe yourself?"

   b. If there are other people in the room ask: "What words would you use to describe him/her/them?"

3. If any people respond with a negative word, here are some ideas for how to respond:

   a. If the person said something negative about themself: "It can be hard sometimes to believe good things about ourselves. I sometimes think negative things about myself too. But they aren't true. And what you said isn't true either. That's why we want to talk about what is true so we can speak it over ourselves every day and live more like who we really are."

   b. If a person said something negative about another group member: "We would never want our place to be an unsafe or hurtful place, but when you said that you made it unsafe and hurtful. What you said isn't true, because _____.

We only want to speak what is true and encouraging to each other. Even if you were joking, it can be harmful. So try again. What is something positive you can say to describe that person?"

4. Once you have your words for each group or family member, come up with a creative way to implement it into the group's daily routine. Here are some suggestions:

a. Write the words on a mirror.

b. Create a chant or "call back" with the person. One person says, "You are–" and the other says, "Smart!" And you work through the list of words that way.

c. For older children, you can encourage them to journal before bed. Have them write down when they felt bad and then cross it off or throw it away and write what is true.

d. Create a group or family mantra or saying that you say together.

Coaching Group or Family Activity

Materials:

-A printed or drawn dice template (To find a template, do a Google search for 'blank dice template')
-Coloring utensils
-Scissors
-Tape or glue

Directions:

1. In this activity you will be creating a six-sided die that represents what each person or family member loves to do. You will use this die to create fun experiences for each other and to teach the group members to listen to each other and care for each other.

2. Say: "We are going to make a die for each other. You are going to ask each other questions, but make sure you listen really well. Their answers are going to help you draw on your die. We are going to use the die whenever we want to make our friend or sibling's day great. But we have to listen to each other to find out what would make their day a great day."

3. Start with the first person and give the other people the list of questions:

    a. Think about the best day in your life. What was it like?
    b. What would make your day the best?
    c. What have your best days been like?
    d. What were you doing?
    e. Who were you with?
    f. How did you feel?

4. Say: "Okay, I hope you listened well because we are going to work together to make _____'s die. We need to think of six things that she/he/they said would make their day. Then you will draw them on the die. So, what

kinds of things would make their day the best?" Brainstorm together and have the other sibling(s) draw on the die.

5. Repeat this for each person.

6. Ask: "What was difficult about this? Was it hard to really listen to the other person?"

Say:

"It can be really difficult to listen to someone else. A lot of times we just want to make the conversation all about us. But today we had to focus on the other person. But wasn't it fun? It will be fun when we get to roll the dice to pick something to do to make their day too. If we do stuff like this in our family or group, we can learn to do it everywhere we go in all of our relationships."

CHAPTER EIGHT: ACCOUNTABILITY

It's difficult to be held accountable, but this is a powerful tool in the ally tool kit. Instead of holding someone accountable without a discussion, consider *inviting them* to be held accountable. It's a subtle shift in language, but one that feels empowering versus constraining. Research has shown that when people set goals like losing weight or exercising more, and are then paired with an accountability partner, they are more likely to be successful in reaching their goals. The same goes for allyship. Invite someone to participate in the journey with you, offer support to one another, and increase your chances of success.

A friend of mine recently started a company with a partner and wanted to give a portion of her profits to a non-profit that she felt passionate about.

She approached the local chapter of Black Lives Matter and was met with resistance. To them, she presented as another White person trying to take advantage and profit off the pain of Black people. While this was not her, or her partner's, intention, they made sure to listen to the feedback and understand why they appeared this way to the organization. The feedback ultimately helped them understand how they could be better allies. As she shared her story with me, I listened, empathized with, "I've been there," and acknowledged the challenge is real. I didn't try to solve the problem for her. I recognized that she just needed someone to lean on and help hold her accountable to her goal of being a better ally.

Allyship can feel lonely, especially during the bumbles and stumbles.

A lot of people engage in one hard conversation or situation and then choose to walk away. They make excuses like, "This is why White people can't say anything about diversity," or "See, I tried." Cancel culture is very real. People look for easy exits and opportunities to find flaws in others to knock them off their pedestals.

As my friend demonstrated to me, she was willing to be held accountable for the mistakes she made, listen to the feedback, and apply it to become a better ally. She didn't make excuses or blame other people, nor did she withdraw completely. She stayed on course and knew this was part of the learning experience.

Real allies stay on course long-term.

Keep Your Ally Radar up

As an ally-in-training, it's important to be aware of opportunities to help people be better around you. This doesn't just mean modeling positive behavior, as discussed in previous chapters. It means bringing awareness to situations where people could have been better allies.

Not too long ago my family and I were discussing US history. We were talking about the problematic behavior of past presidents that we have idealized in textbooks. Many of them owned slaves, were known to father children of slaves (by rape), and one even had dentures made from the teeth of slaves. Some might think that this was normal for that time period, but what we weren't taught was that there were also many hidden White allies who stood against slavery. We only learn about Abraham

Lincoln who supported freeing slaves (opportunistically, to win a war).

Some members of my family defended some past presidents with the statement, "He was a good guy," despite problematic behavior. The point is not for us as allies to decide who's good or who's bad. It's about educating people on the real history, the good and the bad. To only tell the story of the good side in order to keep the bad side hidden keeps the systems that we must fight against as allies in play.

We need to know our real history if we're going to change it.

I left the conversation with my family at that. It's important that we teach our children the real true history, the positive and the negative. They can handle it. It's the only way they will know that we need positive change in the future. I didn't seek to change the minds of my family. I simply shared my point of view and brought awareness to our discussion. That's what allies do with those in their networks. It's not about getting into arguments or changing someone's mind. It's about watching for non-inclusive behavior and mindfully sharing facts and statements that could help correct the course of the conversation.

One of the biggest ways to reinforce accountability with those around you is watching out for microaggressions. We have talked about the harmful effects of microaggressions in previous chapters. Allies understand the harmful effects of these seemingly small, yet painful interactions. Therefore, if they see a microaggression, it is their duty to say something.

Microaggressions are often based on stereotypes. Stereotypes are labels that we place on groups of people that do not necessarily apply to all members of that given group. For example, seventy percent of women are primary caregivers in the US. To make the assumption that a woman of childbearing age has children and is the primary caregiver is more likely to be true than not. However, plenty of women choose not to have children, are not the primary caregiver of their household, or they choose to have a different family structure.

It is harmful to microaggress someone based on a stereotype that we don't know to be true about them—in the example of women as caregivers, the assumption that they are not as involved as a mother (or caregiver) if they have a full-time job and asking, "How do they do it all?" Something we almost never ask men as fathers.

I remember being on an airplane flying first class a few years ago. About ninety percent of the first-class cabin were White men. At this point, I was used to sitting beside them and would partake in the obligatory small talk before turning on my headphones and politely exiting the conversation. I remember the man sitting next to me asking me if I had children. I replied that I did and that she was one year old, to which he said, "That must be so hard."

"No, your judgment is hard," I responded as I fought back tears, but the point was taken. It was devastating to feel like I wasn't a good mom because I worked. I think that working makes me a better mom.

Watch out for stereotypes. That is how our brains operate, recognizing the category and making an assumption based on previous experience with that category, whether it's gender, race, or any dimension of diversity. Don't let your brain shortcut the human element. There is so much more to people than their skin color or gender identity.

Allies keep their radars up by looking for non-inclusive behavior. Here are some all-too-common unhelpful behaviors you may see if you pay attention more:

- Labeling individuals by group traits ("Black culture" vs. Black person).
- Applying stereotypes to individuals (sports, music, dance, food).
- Excluding others because they are different (they would not be interested in...).

Allies pay attention. They don't make excuses for other people's behavior. They interject when necessary to help others learn and be better. One helpful ally exercise that my friend Ericka taught me is to take an inventory of your network. Most of us have "like me" networks due to affinity bias (we naturally gravitate to people like us). Write down the top ten people you choose to spend the most time with (friends, colleagues, etc.).

Allies diversify their networks.

You can look through your phone text messages, call log, emails, or calendar for clues. If you're like me five years ago, you probably have a lot of work to do. I was exclusively hanging out with White women business owners who were mothers. It was like looking in the mirror when spending time with my network. I had to choose to diversify my network to help me see microaggressions and be able to challenge them.

Call People In

In Loretta J. Ross's TED Talk, "Don't Call People Out—Call Them In," she explains the harmful effects of calling people out. Pointing out people's flaws and mistakes in a public situation can be damaging to the ego. People, especially those who are insecure about talking about DEI, usually get defensive, find excuses for their behavior, and retreat from the conversation. Calling people in, however, can be a very helpful tool to help people learn from their not-so-great behavior and get better.

I highly recommend listening to her full talk, especially the end, when she shares the story of her Uncle Frank to explain the concept of calling in. Uncle Frank makes a problematic racist comment at a family dinner and people get uncomfortable. No one says anything, as many microaggressions go uncorrected. Loretta chooses to speak up and say, "I know you to be a good guy, and what you just said is harmful because..." This framing invites Uncle Frank to be better. It doesn't shame or blame him. Everyone around the table sees him as a good person, and her phrasing explains the impact of his behavior. He then has a choice to align his behavior with the good person he is or not. The choice is his.

It is not a matter of if a microaggression occurs; allies are looking proactively for when they occur.

My ally and DEI speaker Bernadette Smith has a really helpful model to call people in. She calls it the Asking, Respect, Connecting (ARC) method:

- Asking is about being open and inquisitive, asking good questions to better understand someone's issues, struggles, or position, and then listening intently.
- Respect is about actively listening and then accepting the data or input provided with an intention to honestly gain insight from it.
- Connecting is then providing appropriate responses and actions.

So, when you get nervous, or your amygdala fires up your fight-or-flight response, take a deep breath and think about a good question you can ask to show curiosity. Balance your tone with real respect for the person and find ways to connect through establishing common ground versus pointing out differences.

Another ally, Kristen Pressner, has a TED Talk, "Are You Biased? I Am." In her talk, she explains being confronted with her own bias with promotion decisions at work, as well as at home, with her own children. She offers a solution: the Flip It to Test It model. The model is helpful in calling people in on their microaggressions.

When you find yourself in a situation where something doesn't feel right, simply flip the genders, races, abilities, sexual orientations, or any dimension of diversity and see if it still makes sense. For instance, you might be surprised by someone's English speaking capabilities and want to compliment them. Before you do that, ask yourself, *Would I make that comment if they were in the majority group?* If not, there is probably some bias at play. If the answer is yes, you are probably safe.

DEI is complex. There is always room for different interpretations. Someone could always interpret something differently than you would. Having a model helps call people in when you might be uncertain of what to say or do. Another model we love to help with candid conversations is the Three D'S model.

The Three D's model stands for Define, Discuss, and Decide. In a conversation where you're trying to hold someone accountable, it's important to define the issue upfront, have a two-way discussion that's truly inclusive of all perspectives, and decide. Often, we leave the conversation emotionally charged and forget to make a decision about what our next step should be. To hold someone accountable, there must be a commitment to a shift in future behavior so that it doesn't happen again.

Here's an example of how the Three D's model could work with a microaggression situation. Let's say you're in a social situation where someone keeps interrupting someone with a diverse background. You practice the Flip It to Test It model after the third interruption and conclude that this would not happen to a White man. Time to invite accountability as an ally.

Make a quick game plan mentally before pulling the person aside with the Three D's:

- Define: What is the issue or challenge? What does success look like? What is the objective or purpose for the conversation?
- Discuss: What is your perspective? What is their perspective? What do you have in common? What is different?
- Decide: What are the commitments? What are the next steps? How can you continue to show up as an ally with them?

Candid DEI conversations have bookends— purpose and accountability.

Simply pausing to reflect and think about mindful questions and facts you could use to support your point of view will help you have a more productive conversation.

Talk Tracks

A White male friend of mine is in the beer distribution industry. The beer distribution industry, like many industries, is comprised mostly of White men. In fact, there's a common joke that they all have beards and beer bellies. Again, the stereotype can often be true, but not always. My friend was working with a retailer to help them diversify their beer shelves. At that time, nearly all of their beer selection was being produced by White male-owned breweries. There happen to be lots of women-owned and Black-owned breweries, but unfortunately, they're not as well represented in the distribution industry, and not as well-known as mainstream brands. This is clearly a problem because White men aren't the only ones who drink beer.

So, my friend saw this as an opportunity to help grow the industry he loves. When he connected the retailer with women- and Black-owned breweries, there was an issue. The retailer had several problematic beer labels on their shelf. For example, there was one with a Black woman's face with the label "Black Chocolate." This reinforces a negative stereotype of Black women being over-sexualized. Needless to say, the new breweries did not want their beer labels to share a shelf with these problematic images.

Instead of letting the issue go unresolved, my friend facilitated a conversation with the brewery that produced the problematic label and they agreed to change the image. They needed that feedback to grow and better understand. It wasn't that they were unwilling to compromise; it was that they did not know how problematic that label was. By inviting more people into the process, you're less likely to make these types of mistakes.

Different perspectives help all of us be better.

Accountability is not a weapon. It's a tool that can help bridge people's lack of understanding. By inviting someone into a conversation to learn, we are helping them be better allies. Some of my favorite ally sentences to start a candid conversation are:

- I used to think that too.
- What did you mean when you said that?
- I get what you were trying to say and here's an idea to consider for next time.
- My perception is...
- Let's do more of X or less of Y.
- What could we do differently next time?
- *Ouch...* (I find that offensive or inapropriate).

All of these I have found to pique people's interests rather than create defensiveness. These phrases, when said genuinely with positive intention, create bridges between different perspectives rather than shame and separation around difference. Practice using a few from time to time and craft your own. They have to feel good for you to use them regularly.

Generally speaking, candid conversations about DEI and microaggressions are best done one-on-one and in person. That is not always possible, yet is the best option if available. If there is high trust in a group, consider speaking candidly as a group as soon as the problem occurs. If there is the ability to pull someone aside and talk privately, do that as soon as possible.

Allies tell people what they need to know to be better.

Being accountable as an ally is like seeing a car wreck. We can drive by without stopping (a bystander) or we can choose to stop the car and offer help (upstander). Allies know that their behavior matters. Not only are they modeling positive behavior for others so that it spreads contagiously, but they are also mindful of course correcting other people and inviting them into accountability.

Allies embrace accountability. Each chapter has a short assessment to better understand where you are and where you want to be as an ally. Consider these assessment results before moving forward with another ally skill set.

Assessment:

- ☐ I look for opportunities to call people in.
- ☐ I identify microaggressions in the moment.
- ☐ I understand bad behaviors and why they cannot continue.
- ☐ I feel comfortable calling people in.
- ☐ I frame discussions with the purpose and end with decisions.
- ☐ I ensure conversations are a two-way dialogue.
- ☐ I use the Flip It to Test It model.
- ☐ I know when to talk privately vs. in front of the group.
- ☐ I tell people what they need to know.
- ☐ I practice speaking up, especially when it is hard.

Accountability Reader Activity

Network Diversity Dimensions Inventory

1. Write down the names of the top ten people you spend the most time with. Look through your phone, emails, calendar, wherever you communicate with people.
2. Categorize your top ten by the following categories: gender, ethnicity, age, socioeconomic status, part of the country, profession, physical ability, and any other category that comes to mind.
3. Process these questions on your own and with a trusted friend:
   a. What is missing from a representation perspective?
   b. Who could you spend more time with?
   c. How could you diversify your network?

Accountability Group or Family Activity

In this activity you will be working together to create a board/interactive elements to put in your home or group space to grow your group's local involvement in DEI. You want to be a facilitator as much as possible and let the rest of the group take the lead on this.

Materials:
- Be creative with how you do this so that it fits your group's routine. Here are some ideas:
    - Corkboard
    - Jar(s)
    - Blackboard/whiteboard
    - Fun paper
    - Frames

Directions:
1. Explain to the group that you want to connect everything you've been learning with the rest of your lives. Explain that you will be creating an interactive board that you will use as a group to plan and create vision and purpose with taking DEI into all aspects of their lives—including the lives of the people around them.
2. Create a way to write down a person in each member's life or just one person. This will be the person you start to engage in conversation with about what you've been learning.
    a. Say: "Let's think of someone in our lives who you want to know about what you've been learning. How can we share with them?"

3. Write down that person's name and then talk about what questions you might ask that person:
   a. What do you want to know more about?
   b. What is holding you back from knowing more or doing more?
   c. Talk about how to share the activities you've been doing as a family.
4. Brainstorm or talk about organizations that support DEI. Talk about these questions:
   a. "Which organization sounds like one you'd like to donate to this month?"
   b. "Where do you want to put the money we save to donate?"
   c. "How can we work to make more money so we can donate more?"
   d. You can change the organization you donate to each month or you can keep the same one—it's up to your group!
5. Talk about how your group can start to bring what they're learning into their schools. Let them brainstorm ways they can and then help with the logistics. Pick a creative way to display their goal for bringing DEI into their school.
6. If an election is coming up, pick a place to write down the name of one candidate who is running. Talk about ways you can learn about this candidate together. Change the name of the candidate every week so your group is learning about someone new together.
7. Pick a time of day to refer to this board. Maybe this is during breakfast, after school, during lunch or dinner, or before bedtime, whatever works best for your group. Have the kids hold the family accountable to talking about how it is going. Make sure the board is interactive so

kids can consistently be engaged in a tactile way (for example, money or chips in a jar, writing, moving parts, adding parts, etc.).

CHAPTER NINE: PRIVILEGE

Privilege is an important word in the ally vocabulary. It's not a word that rolls easily off the tongue (without practice). For many of us, we were taught as young children that privilege was a bad thing or we weren't taught about it at all. There is a huge misconception that acknowledging privilege means you didn't work as hard or you've had it easy your whole life. That's not at all what privilege really means. It's simply acknowledging there are some advantages that you might have by being associated with the majority group.

Privilege is a chance to be an ally.

When we leverage our privilege for good as allies, we help others around us. As a White person working in the DEI space, I'm aware of my White privilege. This means when I speak up about racism or issues that uniquely face people of color, my White voice is heard a bit differently. That may not be fair to people of color, who fully deserve to be heard just the same. Yet, as my friends of color remind me, it doesn't appear as though I have skin in the game. Pun intended.

When a person of color brings up issues of racism, it can appear self-serving to others. I was on a panel for diversity in technology a few years ago. I'll never forget what one of the Black male panelists shared. He shared that he's often the only person of color in rooms personally and professionally. When he acknowledges the unique challenges that he faces because of his skin color, it can be off-putting to White people. However, when a White person brings up the very same issue, people pay attention differently.

That seems so deeply unfair to me. What I learned from him sharing that experience was that my voice can be powerful as an ally, especially when it is used to influence the majority group. I have a well-intentioned White male client who acknowledged that his organization is very much at the infancy of DEI. They are just getting started and don't know what they don't know. After my first presentation to a small group of majority White men, they shared feedback that I had a refreshing approach.

It took me some time to unpack that. It felt like code for "you are like us." Sometimes hearing the message from someone who looks like you is easier to digest. My takeaway: People need to hear this message from all voices—Black, brown, White, straight, gay, non-disabled , those with disabilities. The more we hear the message from a collective chorus of people, the more we bring the full human experience to DEI.

DEI is a human issue.

The "P" Word

Allies speak openly about privilege. They acknowledge that there are many dimensions of privilege. It's not just about race and gender; privilege can come from your family structure, your socioeconomic background, your geography, your industry, and many more.

DIMENSIONS OF DIFFERENCE

I do this exercise regularly with my clients, but it is also helpful for allies at home. Look at the different dimensions of power. The more you associate with the dimensions at the top of the graphic, the more likely you are to have advantages associated with them. If you identify with some of the markers of diversity at the bottom, the less likely you are to have privilege.

I've done this exercise hundreds of times, and without fail, White straight males almost always identify with far more dimensions of power than women and people of color. Of the dozen dimensions listed here, which are by no means an exhaustive list, those in the majority group generally identify with at least ten of them on average. I myself identify with nine of them as a White woman. When people compare notes with people of color or diverse backgrounds, they find a very different situation. More often than not, women of color find themselves with the least amount of privileges.

Privilege is an asset for allies. A friend of mine was not yet an ally when he did his first privilege walk. As a straight, cisgender, White male, he only had one dimension of difference. He wears hearing aids. He describes that moment as his White male epiphany. He had no idea the hardships that other people faced because of diversity before that moment. He was hesitant to support DEI before he understood how many advantages he had simply by being associated with the majority group. He now advocates for DEI openly on his podcast and in places where he speaks. That's the power of understanding privilege. It can help bring people into the DEI conversation.

We didn't choose where we were born or what parents we were born to. That's just luck. When I think about the amount of privilege I have, a lot of it has to do with my parents. I was born in 1982 in Columbus, Ohio to loving parents who had enough money to make sure that I was properly fed, clothed, and cared for. I received a quality education. While we had very low disposable income, I was able to go to college, earn scholarships to pay for the majority of my tuition, and pay off my college debt within five years. I got a job at a Fortune 50 company and had a successful twelve-year corporate career before starting my own business.

I worked hard for a lot of the things I have achieved, but I also know that I was put on a path for success because my parents cared about me and could support me. Not everyone has that experience. When I compare notes with someone who was born in a developing country, an inner city, where parents may not be available due to hardship or scarcity, their story is very different. When you grow up not having enough food or access to education, your life will likely be different. People can work their way out of poverty and out of negative circumstances, but those stories are anomalies. We love the underdog stories of those who, against all odds, find their way to success, but there are *far* more stories of people not breaking free of their circumstances because the systems aren't designed for them.

The more we get comfortable with privilege, the more candid and vulnerable we can be in the DEI conversation. My greatest source of privilege was my mother. Her premature death was a catalyst for me finding my purpose, starting my business, and getting to write books like this one. She always told me my purpose in life was to help women. I came to realize what she really meant was people like me, and different from me, who deserve better. Because of the privileges that she granted me and the deep love I received as a child, I am able to do work deeply aligned with my purpose. That's a privilege I have to acknowledge every day.

Allies show up every day.

One of the biggest risks I face in writing this book is people thinking that I'm whitesplaining DEI. That's not my intention, yet that could be a fair perception of others. If that's the biggest risk that I have to take in leveraging my privilege for good, that's a pretty small risk. Ask yourself that same question: What's the biggest risk I am taking by trying to be an ally? Chances are the benefits far outweigh the risks.

Individual vs. Systemic Change

Race and gender are social constructs. Before White people decided to enslave people of color, we looked at each other as human beings. We may have been from different tribes or regions, but we had a general mutual respect for one another. Until one day, someone decided that light skin made you superior, and dark skin made you inferior.

Racism doesn't make sense. When we talk openly with our children about racism, they have genuine bewilderment about how the color of your skin can dictate how you're treated. That is because, underneath our skin, we are all very much the same. The only real difference is the melanin level in our skin. Over time, White people found reasons to justify their mistreatment of people of color, ranging from wild claims about brain size to animalistic tendencies. While all have since been refuted, these were lies told to support white supremacy.

Today, white supremacy looks very different. It's not wearing a KKK cloak or declaring yourself a white nationalist. It's more about simply believing that the white race is somehow superior to other races. White supremacy is nuanced. It could be subtle, like not being attracted to people of different races or believing a child of color has innate behavioral problems. None of these differences are biological; they are socialized.

I attended a high school graduation party last summer and offered my congratulations to the graduate. Somehow the subject of gender came up in our conversation. They identify as gender nonbinary and openly declared "gender is a construct." I was taken aback by this astute observation, and as I thought about it, I arrived at the same conclusion—of course it's a construct. Sure, there are biological differences between men and women. However, many of the differences are socialized and learned. Girls are not innately bossy; boys are not born leaders. Confidence and gender expression is learned over time. By teaching our girls to be pleasing and take care of the needs of others before their own, to be seen and not heard, we are conditioning them based on gender.

As we acknowledge the systems that support the majority group that tend to be less supportive of women, people of color, LGBTQ+, and those with disabilities, we are all playing a role in the system. Some of us are benefiting from the unfair advantages that we receive by being associated with the majority group and others are being disadvantaged by not having access to those same opportunities.

Self-awareness is key as an ally. Acknowledging your own points of privilege doesn't make you a bad person. If you identify as straight and cisgender and attend a gay pride parade, or speak openly about your support of LGBTQ+ youth and advocating for the gay community, what are you losing? One of our most primal needs as humans is to help others. It's how we earned the right to be a part of our tribes as hunters and gatherers. Today, it's how relationships are formed. We are a social species and are not meant to be alone. Helping others who have less privilege than you ultimately helps you too.

Helping others is a deep, primal human need.

We've covered a lot of ways that you can show up as an individual in the DEI conversation through the tools in this book—vulnerability, empathy, curiosity, coaching, and more. Allyship is most powerful when individuals leverage their privilege to disrupt the systems that benefit them. That could be advocating for tax dollars to be spent on developing communities of color or housing programs that support people with different socioeconomic statuses. It can feel like you're losing something as an ally, that somehow by acknowledging your privilege you might be giving up some of your advantages, but that is not the case.

Allyship is not a zero-sum game.

A lot of White men share that they feel like they are rooting against themselves by supporting DEI. It is not about losing your privilege; it is about sharing your privilege with others. By evening out the playing field for everyone, you stand to benefit from the equality that's created. When we have systems keeping certain people down and certain people up, we are not as innovative, strong, or optimal. We're all losing when we leave these systems unchecked.

In the disability community, the curb-cut effect is a well-known social phenomenon. When we lowered curbs to support people in wheelchairs, there was a ripple effect to other groups of people—people that push baby strollers, bicyclists, and small children. In creating a better environment for people with disabilities, we also created a better environment for all people. Similar to the concept that a rising tide lifts all boats, when we make systems equitable for some, they tend to benefit us all.

Different Starting Points

I attended a Women in Technology conference many years ago. It was there that I participated in my first privilege exercise. Everyone formed a circle and had a sticker and a scale behind them. As the facilitator shared statements, if you agreed, you moved your sticker up a notch, or if you disagreed with the statement, you moved your sticker down a notch. After about twenty or so questions, the facilitator asked everyone to move to the side to show the group where their sticker was placed.

The statements ranged from childhood experiences, living circumstances, access to education, housing, and politics. As we scanned the room, it was quite obvious that the White women placed much higher on the scale than women of color. The White women candidly shared that they felt embarrassed and ashamed of their privilege. The women of color felt embarrassed and confused by their lack of privilege but had seen it as a strength to overcome obstacles to get to where they are.

There are several different versions of this privilege activity. Many items on this list are excerpted with permission from *Better Allies: Everyday Actions to Create Inclusive, Engaging Workplaces* by Karen Catlin.

Consider some of these questions below:

- My parent(s) or caregiver(s) attended college.
- I attended college.
- I have never skipped a meal because there was no food in the house.
- I am a White man.
- I have all of my cognitive and physical abilities.
- I have a college degree.
- I attended an elite university.
- I was born in the United States.
- English is my first language.
- I never have felt passed over for a job based on my gender, ethnicity, age, or sexual orientation.
- I do not feel excluded from key social or networking opportunities because of my gender, ethnicity, age, or sexual orientation.
- I have not been asked to do menial office tasks that colleagues of another gender are not asked to do.
- I can speak openly about my significant other.
- I feel I can actively and effectively contribute to meetings I attend.
- I have recently received feedback about a skill I need to grow my career.
- I can talk about politically oriented extracurricular activities without fear of judgment from colleagues.
- I have a partner who takes on a large share of household and family responsibilities.

- I have never been called a "diversity hire."
- I have never been mistaken as a member of the catering staff at an event.
- I have never received an unwanted sexual advance at work.
- I feel safe being my full self at work.
- I am not concerned about losing my job because of my financial situation.
- I am able to join in out-of-office lunches or after-work social activities because the cost of these activities is not a concern to me.
- I grew up with a computer in the home.
- I read story books as a kid with characters who looked like me.
- I grew up with mayors, politicians, and a president who looked like me.
- I can walk past a construction site without being stared at or catcalled.
- I was not embarrassed as child to have friends at my home.
- I go to meetings where people look like me.
- I have friends at work who look and think like me.

This exercise is not about keeping score. It's not about who has more privilege or who has less privilege. It is not about comparing the pain we've experienced due to our lack of privilege. It isn't a contest either. No one wins or gets a privilege gold star. Comparing suffering doesn't help DEI. It's about all of us, privileged and underprivileged, coming together as allies. There is no us vs. them. It is about truly *seeing* each other and being good humans together.

We are stronger together.

I was teaching an Unpacking Racism course last year and a White, straight male who happened to be from the South did this privilege exercise. He, like most White males, assessed a high level of privilege. Part of the exercise was to compare notes with someone different than himself. He chose one of his counterparts, a Black woman. His counterpart had privileges growing up that he did not share from a socioeconomic status, but he quickly realized that none of the disadvantages that he had faced in his life were because of his skin color. The exact opposite was true for his colleague.

This was a real moment of clarity and self-awareness for him. He had no idea that he was afforded many privileges even though he worked very hard to get to where he was in his life. As he shared the story with the rest of the class, tears brimmed in his eyes and he said, "I've got to do better." That's a critical moment in the ally journey. Acknowledging you're not perfect and that you didn't ask for the privileges you were given. Nonetheless, you're going to use your privilege to help other people and be better.

I teach the Unpacking Racism Certification course with my ally and co-facilitator Ericka. Ericka is a Black woman and has shared a tremendous amount about her lived experience as a person of color. Although I will never fully understand her experience, Ericka's perspective has shifted how I see race completely. When we go for walks together in White-dominated areas, I see how people welcome me. So much of my privilege is associated with freedom of movement. I can go a lot more places and feel safer than Ericka, and that is not fair.

Ericka's favorite way to explain privilege is the moving walkway analogy. If you think about a moving walkway, there are two lanes. One lane for people who are standing, the other lane for people who are walking. Privilege is like being on the moving walkway and being able to walk

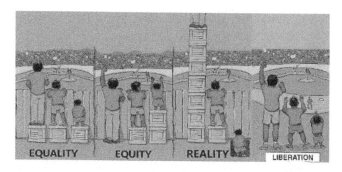

Liberation

https://ces101fall2018.files.wordpress.com/2018/09/equity-equality-liberation-reality-liberation

freely. Not having privilege is like being on the moving walkway and having to stand still. We're all on the walkway of life together but some of us are moving faster than others.

As you can see in the graphic, equality is treating everyone equally and expecting a different result. This is similar to the concept of insanity, doing the same thing and expecting a different outcome. Most well-intended allies say they believe in equality. I myself used to say that. What I've come to realize is that *equity* is necessary to disrupt the systems that keep people down. Those who have the least amount of privilege need different levels of support to achieve equality. That means providing tools and meeting people where they're at and distributing resources by need, rather than the same resources to all.

This graphic has many iterations. I personally like the four boxes because it includes reality and liberation. The reality is people with diverse backgrounds have the deck stacked against them, just like the boxes stacked against them. It feels like you're trying but you're not breaking through that invisible wall. Liberation can only happen when we achieve systemic change.

As an ally, think about the systems you can influence. Did you or do your children have access to a privileged education system based on property taxes? Can you easily vote for people who will represent you well? Do you have access to affordable housing? Do you trust the healthcare system? If you said yes to any of these questions, those are systems that you can impact as an ally. Get informed at a local level and think about how you can influence change so that all people have equitable access to these systems.

As you flex from individual action to systemic change, it is important to work across all the dimensions of diversity.

"Intersectionality is a lens through which you can see where power comes and collides, where it interlocks and intersects. It's not simply that there's a race problem here, a gender problem here, and a class or a LBGTQ problem there. Many times, that framework erases what happens to people who are subject to all of these things." Kimberle Crenshaw

DEI is intersectional.

As allies, we can't look at it from one dimension, but rather as a collective where each dimension has the ability to intersect with other dimensions. That makes it challenging to disrupt. Knowing that women of color, or those who are gay with disabilities, experience multiple dimensions of difference can be difficult to comprehend as an ally (who doesn't experience one or more of those intersections) but so very critical to fighting the systems that disadvantage people in multiple ways. I think of intersectionality like tethering. It's impossible to separate the multiple factors at play. That means for women of color it's impossible to show up as a woman one minute and a Black person the next moment. Their experiences happen simultaneously.

Allies know who they are and who they're not. They're very clear about the strengths that they have. They leverage their privilege for good. They are aware of the areas that could be weaknesses or opportunities to grow and get better. Privilege is a chance to be an ally. Each chapter has a short assessment to better understand where you are and where you want to be as an ally. Consider these assessment results before moving forward with another ally skill set.

Assessment:

- ☐ I know who I am and who I am not.
- ☐ I acknowledge my privilege.
- ☐ I see privilege as a way to help others.
- ☐ I know my dimensions of power.
- ☐ I understand power structures keep certain people up and other people down.
- ☐ I understand that White privilege is real.
- ☐ I understand that gender and race are social constructs.
- ☐ I understand the differences between equity and equality.
- ☐ I understand what intersectionality is.
- ☐ I want to leverage my privilege for positive systemic change.

Privilege Reader Activity

Privilege Exercise

Complete the following privilege exercise. The purpose of this activity is getting a better understanding of your sources of privilege and those that you know. Privilege is not a bad thing; it is a chance to be an ally for someone different than you.

For each statement, put a + sign if you agree or a – sign if you disagree. Tally your total + signs and – signs at the conclusion.

1. My parent(s) or caregiver(s) attended college.
2. I attended college.
3. I have never skipped a meal because there was no food in the house.
4. I am a White man.
5. I have all of my cognitive and physical abilities.
6. I have a college degree.
7. I attended an elite university.
8. I was born in the United States.
9. English is my first language.
10. I never have felt passed over for a job based on my gender, ethnicity, age, or sexual orientation.
11. I do not feel excluded from key social or networking opportunities because of my gender, ethnicity, age, or sexual orientation.

12. I have not been asked to do menial office tasks that colleagues of another gender are not asked to do.

13. I can speak openly about my significant other.

14. I feel I can actively and effectively contribute to meetings I attend.

15. I have recently received feedback about a skill I need to grow my career.

16. I can talk about politically-oriented extracurricular activities without fear of judgment from colleagues.

17. I have a partner who takes on a large share of household and family responsibilities.

18. I have never been called a "diversity hire."

19. I have never been mistaken as a member of the catering staff at an event.

20. I have never received an unwanted sexual advance at work.

21. I feel safe being my full self at work.

22. I am not concerned about losing my job because of my financial situation.

23. I haven't been unable to join in out-of-office lunches or after-work social activities because of the cost.

24. I grew up with a computer in the home

25. I read story books as a kid with characters who looked like me.

26. I grew up with mayors, politicians, and/or a president who looked like me.

27. I can walk past a construction site without being stared at or cat-catcalled.

28. I was not embarrassed as child to have friends at my home.
29. I go to meetings where people look like me
30. I have friends at work who look and think like me.

___ Total – signs   ___ Total + signs

When you finish, process these questions:

    a. What shifted for you?
    b. How are you seeing your life differently now?
    c. How can you start to use your privilege for positive change?
    d. What statements were surprising to see on this list as indicators of privilege?

Privilege Group or Family Activity 1

Group Privilege Exercise:

1. Once you have completed the privilege activity on your own, lead your family or group through this version. You will probably want to do this together so children understand each statement.

2. Say: "The purpose of this activity is for you to get a better understanding of your sources of privilege. Privilege is like an advantage you have. It's usually something you didn't earn—you have it just because of where you were born, how you grew up, what you look like, and other things you didn't control. Privilege is not a bad thing; it is a chance to be an ally for someone different than you."

3. Read and discuss each statement with your children. For each statement, put a + sign if they agree or a – sign if they disagree.

4. Tally your total + signs and – signs at the conclusion.

5. Discuss these questions:
    a. What was surprising to you?
    b. Was there anything on the list that you thought everyone else experienced too? Something you thought was "normal" for all kids?
    c. How does this make you live or think differently now?

1. My parent(s) or caregiver(s) attended college.
2. I have never skipped a meal because there was no food in the house.
3. I am a White male.
4. I have all of my cognitive and physical abilities.
5. I am in a school with a majority of students and teachers who look like me.
6. I am able to attend any school I want
7. My parents talk about me going to college one day.
8. I was born in the United States.
9. English is my first language.
10. I never have felt passed over for a sport or activity based on my gender, ethnicity, age, or sexual orientation.
11. I do not feel excluded from friendships or social events because of my gender, ethnicity, age, or sexual orientation.
12. I can speak openly about my parents/family.
13. I feel I can actively speak up in class.
14. I feel safe being my full self at school.
15. I am not concerned about my parents because of their financial situation.
16. I haven't had to say "no" to a social situation because my parents couldn't pay for it.
17. I have a computer in the home.
18. I read story books with characters who look like me.

19. I watch movies and television shows with lead characters who look like me.

20. I see mayors, politicians, and/or a president who looks like me.

21. I am not embarrassed to have friends at my home.

22. I go to activities and sports where people look like me.

23. I have friends at school who look and talk like me.

___ Total – signs   ___ Total + signs

Privilege Group or Family Activity 2

Materials:
- A computer, phone, or smart TV with access to YouTube
- **Barbie Racism Video** (To find this video, search on YouTube for 'barbie racism video')

Directions:

1. Watch the Barbie Racism video together as a family or group.
2. Discuss the following questions together:
   a. What situations were unfair? Why?
   b. How would you respond to a friend if they shared things like that?
   c. What could you do to prevent or stop things like that happening to people in your life?

CHAPTER TEN: INSPIRATION

Now that you have assembled your ally tool kit, this chapter is dedicated to helping you set out on your journey. I hope the stories and techniques shared in this chapter inspire you to go out into the world and be a better ally to those around you.

Self-awareness is the gift of understanding that we can give to ourselves. Understanding our desires, assets, limitations, and the way we process experiences enables us to be better people as we interact with the world around us. Self-awareness also brings forth our authenticity. If you have a genuine desire to care for others, make our world better for all, or use your privilege for good, your authenticity will shine through your work as an ally and inspire others to join in.

Allies inspire others to be allies around them.

As humans, we hate to feel alone and isolated. It is so important to remember, especially when things get tough, that you are not alone on your ally journey. There are so many of us out there, and while our individual work might seem small, collectively we are making a difference. What keeps me strong and inspires me to keep going, on the hardest days, is seeing evidence of the other allies in the world. Even the smallest gesture, like seeing an inspirational post on social media, reminds me why this work matters.

Even though things are heading in the right direction, there is still a long way to go before we achieve equality for all. In fact, it is unlikely that we will achieve equality in our lifetime, or possibly our children's. This is difficult to accept but important to realize, as we need to carry forward this conversation with our children and the next generation of allies. This problem will not solve itself and there is a lot of work to be done to right the wrongs of our past.

It is a disservice to our children if we raise them to be colorblind or allow our girls to believe that they can do anything. We believe we are being hopeful and shielding them from the harsh realities of the world, but what we are really doing is giving them a false sense of the world, which can be jarring once they finally enter it as adults (much like the shock I experienced when entering the workplace). We need to be honest with our children, friends, and family, knowing the truth will empower them to join us as allies for change.

For elementary-school-aged children, sharing simple situations, facts, and encouraging curiosity are key. By the time they become teenagers, most adolescents stop asking caregivers for advice and instead begin to rely on their peers. As an ally, ask and listen; avoid the compulsion to immediately advise. Remember, you don't have to be the expert on everything that should come up. You can always learn and grow alongside your children. With the internet, everything is at our fingertips. Our most important job is to prepare them for adulthood, and DEI is going to be a part of that.

Deb Dagit, a DEI consultant and ally, shared, *"There is kind of a magic age for learning DEI concepts at eleven years old or around fifth grade. Before that, it's difficult for most kids developmentally to fully engage in empathy and the concept of different lived experiences. Before eleven, there is curiosity about difference. Kids will say things like, 'I don't care if they're different from me, we both enjoy playing soccer, singing, so we are friends.' After that magic age, they tend to care more about what their peers think and it may become difficult for anyone other than a peer to influence them. Right around eleven they are still curious and at the same time able to walk in another person's shoes. They want to understand and care about others lived experience."*

The tween years are an optimal window for DEI conversations.

Last December, my eight-year-old daughter, Jane, asked me about Kwanzaa. At the time, I honestly didn't know that much about it. Together we googled Kwanzaa and learned that it is a week-long celebration of African heritage, unity, and culture. It was a great opportunity for me to demonstrate curiosity with her, and I learned something new. I am by no means a perfect ally. These conversations help us be better allies, together.

Lindsay Lyons, DEI educational consultant, shared a practice that she uses to teach adults how to talk with children about DEI. She calls them "redo scenarios" and suggests that we say: *"This (situation) happened, and I feel ___ about it. Let's talk about how we could do it better next time."*

This type of language allows the child the space to uncover how a situation makes them feel and to arrive at the solution on their own, which is essentially coaching.

In situations that may seem difficult or uncomfortable to approach discussing DEI, it can be helpful to refer back to your ally vision that we brainstormed back in Chapter One.

Your Ally Vision

Having a strong ally vision helps us stay on course, especially when we make mistakes. Manifestation is the intentional habit of reminding yourself of your beliefs, goals, and dreams. When I wrote my first book, *Pivot Point*, many years ago, I developed a habit of writing positive affirmations on sticky notes and placing them around my office. Messages to inspire me that read "People will enjoy reading my book," "The world needs to hear this message," and "I am an author," hung all around for me to see as I was writing. The habit of manifesting those beliefs, when I had not yet written a book, helped me overcome the daunting and paralyzing feelings that many first-time authors face.

Positive affirmations can be helpful for those whom we want to help be better allies. Simply complete these sentences:

- I am striving to be a __ ally.
- I commit to being a __ ally.
- I want to be a __ ally.

This habit can help anyone who wants to be an ally in the DEI conversation. Manifest the type of ally you want to be and envision your success. We all make mistakes and feel overwhelmed and embarrassed that we don't know all of the answers, but feel comfort in the fact that you are doing your part in a very important mission.

Allies need tools.

Nate Turner, DEI advocate and ally, shared with me a visualization exercise that he does regularly with his allies. They create their own Wikipedia pages together. Consider these prompts for a similar activity with your family:

- I want people to remember me as...

- What three words do I want people to use to describe me?
- What's most important to me in the world and why?

We often ask our children the question, "What do you want to be when you grow up?" Instead, Nate argues we should be asking, "What type of person do you want to be?" or "What impact do you want to create in the world?" or "How do you see yourself in the future?" Most children don't know what they want to be until after they have completed their education, or much later in life. It took me until I was thirty-one years old to figure out what career I wanted to pursue, but the kind of person I want to be has remained the same since my childhood.

We gain more clarity about the actions we need to take when we actualize who we want to be, how we want to live, and where we want to go in life. Sometimes our allies see what is in us before we realize ourselves. Think about how you can help those you are an ally to by showing them what they might not yet see in themselves.

Allies put up the mirror for us to better see ourselves.

Successful allies have a vision for success, practice their skills, and are always ready to step up when they are signaled.

Ally Signaling

I'm not a huge fan of DC's Batman, but I can't resist using the Bat-Signal as a metaphor for ally signaling. You see, the people of Gotham, who Batman serves and protects, shine the Bat-Signal into the night sky when they need his help, calling Batman into action. When we witness microaggressions, harmful comments or behavior, observe someone being marginalized, or are approached by inquiring minds, we are being signaled into action as an ally. We need others to see us as an ally to rely on when times are tough, someone who can observe, listen, and guide.

Allyship also means that we have to put a signal out too, to let others know that we are learning to understand and that we are striving to be our most inclusive.

There are many ways that you can signal that you are a developing ally. One example is sharing your pronouns. For ally signals to be effective, they must be intentional and consistent over time. What signals do you want to send as an ally? Consider these positive behaviors to model as an ally:

- De-center the majority group when talking about history or recent events.
- Diversify your network.
- Display a sign of support for inclusivity in your yard or personal spaces.
- Follow diverse voices on social media; interact and share their posts.
- Teach the real history to the next generation of little allies.

An example of de-centering whiteness and teaching real history is in the story of Ruby Bridges. Ruby Bridges was the first African American child to desegregate an all-White elementary school in New Orleans in 1960. When her story is shared, we often focus on the angry White parents and mobs who surrounded the school in her first few months. By centering whiteness, we lose focus on Ruby as the heroine. De-center the negative images and refocus on her positive image as an ally.

When my daughter was born eight years ago, I vowed to never let her play with Barbies. With that toy company I saw a lack of diversity and an unrealistic portrayal of beauty. Now, eight years later, I feel that Barbie has made a lot of progress and Jane has both the Rosa Parks and Helen Keller Barbies (and many more). Both dolls facilitated opportunities to discuss Rosa's courage with the Montgomery Bus Boycott and Helen Keller's diversity story as a way to showcase overcoming adversity.

Allies recognize and reward positive behavior.

Another way to signal that you are an aspiring ally is to recognize the positive behavior of children. If your child plays with another child who is different from them at the playground, that's an opportunity to recognize their positive behavior. If your child picks out a toy that resembles someone different from themself, that's an opportunity to appreciate differences. If your child wants to watch a movie that features a protagonist different from them, that too is a door to a conversation.

Mita Mallick, head of inclusion, equity, and impact at Carta, shared with me this story about allyship at home. *"One of the lessons I am trying to instill in my children is that we can vote with our wallets. Who we choose to support and how we support them matters. This means supporting our local shops and restaurants in our communities, particularly those owned by individuals from historically underrepresented groups. For my daughter's recent birthday, we were invited to send goodie bags for her class. Instead of buying jars of Play-Doh off Amazon, we had a discussion about who we could choose to support. We decided to give each of her classmates a box of cookies from Partake Foods, a Black-woman-owned business led by Denise Woodard. Whether it's five dollars or five hundred dollars we are spending, how we choose to spend that money matters and can have a ripple effect on our ecosystem."*

Mita often posts on social media showcasing great stories, organizations, and people's inclusive behaviors. I recently had a chance to meet Mita on Zoom and she shared she just launched a podcast focusing on elevating the voices of women of color. Her children are an inspiration for her work as a woman of color. She shares candid photos of them, conversations, and vulnerabilities that she has as a mom who also has a corporate career. Mita's voice matters in this world, and I am thankful she keeps showing up, even when it is hard, especially when it is not easy. Her voice inspires me to keep talking.

Representation matters.

DEI consultant and ally Jennifer Brown recently co-authored the book *Beyond Diversity*. The book showcases positive examples of DEI in film, education, store design, and all aspects of our personal and professional lives. In talking with Jennifer about her book, she said allies can look for examples every day of inclusion and non-inclusion. By keeping your ally radar up in all aspects of your life, and sharing those examples with others, you're helping model and teach others how to be more inclusive. People need positive and negative examples to learn from.

Allies create space for others.

A DEI advocate and hopeful ally, Daniel Juday calls himself a "space creator." In connecting with Daniel to learn how straight, White men can support inclusive behavior at home, he shared, *"We teach our kids what is comfortable and what is uncomfortable by our own actions."* Everyday experiences like volunteering, casual conversations about observations, or watching a movie or documentary together are all examples of modeling and creating space for DEI conversations. So are building cross-cultural friendships. Oftentimes we use the term "exposure" when talking about opportunities to teach our children about new cultures or experiences. Daniel prefers the term engagement over exposure. He says, *"We show our children that these are our friends. We aren't 'exposing' them to different cultures by inviting people of different backgrounds into our home. This isn't about saying 'look how different these people are.' These are generative and reciprocal relationships we're engaged in. We always get as much or more than we give. We learn, laugh, cry, and grow together. We engage."*

The Long Game

Allies realize DEI is a long game, which is hard because humans are wired for instant gratification. We like certainty over uncertainty. We prefer short-term guarantees over seeing better results long-term. There was a famous marshmallow test performed with children at Stanford in 1972. In the study, the children were offered a choice between one small, instant reward or two small rewards if they waited. The researcher left the room for about fifteen minutes and then returned with their preferred treat, a marshmallow. In follow-up studies, the researchers found that children who were able to wait longer for their rewards tended to have better life outcomes.

Allies know to resist the temptation to just settle for smaller wins when the longer-term, bigger picture matters more. Be sure to remind yourself of the feeling of satisfaction of achieving a long-term goal, rather than the short-term temporary dopamine rush when you achieve a smaller goal.

I make it a priority to network with people of color, those with disabilities, and allies in the LGBTQ+ communities. One of the questions I like to ask is, "What can I be doing more to signal that I want to be an ally for people like you?" The most common response I get is to keep talking about DEI. Talking is a start, but walking the talk is much more important, and continuing to show up and engage in this conversation is meaningful. You may think that it's just your voice amongst a sea of opposition, but it's our individual voices that matter.

Allies know their voices matter.

An ally of mine has a family journal. They take turns at the dinner table each night sharing what they failed at that day. They acknowledge as a family together what they will do better next time. My family is not so daring. We generally share our favorite part of the day. However, I believe that switching it up and instead sharing our mistakes would make us vulnerable and encourage a growth mindset, teaching our children to take chances. That's why I like trading stories of allyship with others. Sometimes their tools work for me, and sometimes they don't. Worst-case scenario, I learn something new.

Allyship can be a long and arduous journey, and it is crucial to stay inspired and informed to keep showing up. In writing this book, I wanted to recognize my allies and share their stories. I hope they inspired you and gave you some ideas on how to be a better ally too. If you are uncertain of where to start, consider these ideas to inspire others to be allies around you:

- Recognize your allies—tell them the impact they have had on you to motivate them to continue to support you and DEI
- Do it (even when you are afraid)—have the conversation you have been wanting to have with someone who may not 'get it' yet

- Share your story—all of us have a diversity story and set of unique lived experiences
- Engage more allies—invite others into the conversation
- Ask for help from your allies—be specific with ways people around you can be more supportive and keep using your voice for positive change

Allyship is a journey without a destination. Thank you for showing up.

Assessment:

- ☐ I know my ally vision.
- ☐ I share my ally vision with others.
- ☐ I will stay committed to diversity and inclusion even when it is hard.
- ☐ I see a future that is more inclusive.
- ☐ I signal to others the changes I want to see.
- ☐ I recognize the positive behaviors of others.
- ☐ I understand DEI is a long game.
- ☐ I set expectations for others to be inclusive.
- ☐ I share my diversity story.
- ☐ I recognize and ask for help from my allies.

Inspiration Reader Activity

Ally Vision Journal

1. Find a way to keep a journal and a way to process regularly with someone you trust in your life. Reflect on these questions as you consider your DEI journey:

    a. What is going well in your journey?

    b. How are you becoming a better ally for others?

    c. How are you diversifying your network?

    d. How are you having more candid conversations about DEI?

    e. What differences have you noticed with people in your life around DEI?

Inspiration Group or Family Activity

Materials:
-The following list of questions saved somewhere, like your phone, so that you have them handy when needed.

Directions:
1. Use the following list of questions and conversation starters to keep the conversation about DEI and allyship consistent in your household or group space. Ask a question or two in the car, during playtime, at the dinner table, over breakfast, on a walk, before bed, etc.

a. Were you an ally to someone today? Tell me about it.

b. Did you see someone getting bullied and treated badly today? Tell me about it.

c. Who did you play with at recess? What did you do together?

d. Is there anyone new you want to invite over to our house?

e. What do you wish people understood about you? What do you want me to know about you?

f. Was there a time you felt like you couldn't be yourself? Or was there a time you felt like you needed to change part of yourself? Tell me about it.

g. Pick someone whose day you want to make. Let's talk about how we can do that!

CONCLUSION: MAY THE FORCE BE WITH YOU

I believe we can all learn to be better allies for one another over time. Much like my imperfect background in allyship, I have learned by making mistakes, bumbling, stumbling, and people calling me in to be better. Let's not wait for perfection; let's welcome people who care about diversity, equity, and inclusion and equip them with the tools to be successful.

Accept progress over perfection.

DEI is a long game, but if more of the majority group are more involved in the conversation, especially those with privilege and power, we will move more quickly. The challenges we face are living in a culture where we see differences but don't acknowledge them. We instill the myth of meritocracy, and we do not prioritize the education of our real histories. We want to be allies but hesitate to speak openly about DEI in our personal spaces out of fear.

"Fear is the path to the dark side. Fear leads to anger. Anger leads to hate. Hate leads to suffering." Yoda

Allies get comfortable with the uncomfortable. They know that fear is part of the process, and they show up even when they are afraid. They push against the status quo, and they question what is "normal." They resist the temptation to have the answers, go into protector mode, and be in control.

We cannot kick the can to the next generation of allies.

Our biases are formed during childhood, and as we learned in earlier chapters, we are most capable of understanding the complexities of DEI in our tweens. If we do not supply the next generation of little allies with better information, they are more likely to repeat the same mistakes of previous generations.

Look for Positive Ally Role Models

Chances are, you're a better ally than you realize. If you're still having doubts about having DEI conversations, that's completely normal and you aren't alone. I too have those twinges of doubt on a regular basis. When this happens, I remind myself that it's my privilege that grants me the choice to show up and that others don't have that same option.

To stay on the ally journey and avoid the dangers of performative allyship, it's important to surround yourself with people who model the behaviors you want to see more of. Take an inventory of your network and find out where your gaps are by evaluating those you spend most of the time with personally and professionally.

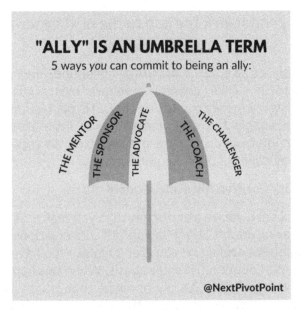

All of us have some affinity bias and spend time with people like us. We gravitate towards the similarity over difference, but it doesn't have to be that way. Simply intervening with that bias and intentionally diversifying who you spend time with can help you be a better ally. It has to be intentional and consistent over time to work.

"You will find only what you bring in." Yoda

Showing up when DEI is in the news cycle is not enough. I have oversimplified DEI issues through comments on social media, for example, and have gotten called in. While my intentions were good, the impact of my words had the opposite effect. When times get tough, I remind myself that people who look like me may have caused a lot of pain to people who experience the adversity of diversity. I am a White woman, and White women, like me, have to do better.

Allies show up in personal and professional spaces.

As I was writing this book, Dictionary.com recognized allyship as the 2021 word of the year. Although the word has been around since the mid 1800s, it became a leading search term in 2020 and 2021 following the long overdue social justice movement. It appears as though people are very curious about allyship, as they don't know what it means. I hope this book has given you a lot of practical ideas to be a better ally at home and at work.

Meet People Where They Are at

Not all of us are allies. Spending time with the people who don't get it and don't want to get it can deplete our energy. We're much better off spending time with the magic middle who wants to get it and don't get it yet. Empathize with people, assist in providing them with resources to learn and grow, and help them understand that their voice is needed in DEI.

"If no mistake you have made, losing you are. A different game you should play." Yoda

The magic middle will say and do harmful things occasionally. They don't know what they don't know. Rather than jumping in with judgment, practice these ally skills. Empathize, manage your emotions, and coach them to success. You'll be a better human for it and so will they.

Stay on the Journey

"Do or do not. There is no try." Yoda

Several years ago, when I wrote my book *ONE: How Male Allies Support Women for Gender Equality*, I conducted an online poll to figure out what the right word was to describe men who support women at work. None of the terms were perfect, and honestly, I didn't like any of them myself. We tested "ambassadors," "allies," "advocates," and "accomplices." Overwhelmingly, people picked the fifth option as their favorite—no word at all. "Allies" came in second, so we went with that even though it was imperfect.

If there were more allies, we wouldn't need a word for it. Instead we would need language to describe positive behavior. While on the ally journey, we need to demonstrate the behaviors that we want to see more of. Many people describe allyship very differently.

Dictionary.com defines allyship as:

1) The status or role of a person who advocates and actively works for the inclusion of a marginalized or politicized group in all areas of society, not as a member of that group but in solidarity with its struggle and point of view and under its leadership. Genuine allyship does not come with special recognition—we do not get awards for confronting issues people have to live with every day.

2) The relationship or status of persons, groups, or nations associating and cooperating with one another for a common cause or purpose.

I prefer simple definitions that I can explain to a child or in a casual conversation with a friend. I define allyship as supporting someone who's different from you. It could be being a friend, a mentor, a coach, a trusted advisor, or a listener to someone of a different ethnicity, race, religion, sexual orientation, gender, ability, or more. The key is you are doing it for them, and not for your own benefit.

DEI starts with U.

If you want positive change in the world, the only person you can one hundred percent control is yourself. Fair warning, it is easy to veer off course. I have to remind myself to stay accountable to allyship, and I do it for a living. I plan to hold myself accountable for DEI by following these journal prompts from Chapter One:

- How did I use my voice?
- What fears did I face?
- What conversations did I have that were helpful?
- What am I thankful for someone sharing with me?
- What did I learn that I cannot unknow?
- What is shifting in me?
- How am I connecting with my ally why?
- What steps have I taken to be closer to my ally vision?
- What is one way I hope to grow more?
- How can I share my journey with others?

Consider completing these journal prompts a few times a week or even every day. Reflect on your responses and see where your strengths and opportunities are. Simply processing your thoughts intentionally and consistently will shift your own behavior over time, enabling you to model what good actions look like to others. Invite others to also be held accountable. Find a trio where you can take turns sharing, processing, and interpreting your journeys together.

Research shows that when we have a plan our chances of success nearly double. With a plan in hand, it's much easier to manifest and visualize success as an ally. A good plan is simple and has an ally vision, goals, and key ninety-day actions. Consider our ally plan template and post it somewhere where you'll see it often. I regularly do an ally vision board exercise every January and I put it where I keep my workout equipment in my office closet. I see it almost every day and it reminds me to stay on course as an ally.

Ally Action Plan Template

Vision:

Goals:

1.
2.
3.

Action Step	Activities Included	Resources Needed	Timeline
1.	•		
2.	•		
3.	•		

I believe in you. Thank you for staying on this journey. My hope is that by practicing these key ally skills, you will model the change you want to see in others and spread active allyship to those around you. Cheers to your successful journey—may the Force be with you.

Assessment:

- ☐ **I commit to staying on journey.**
- ☐ **I understand this work will never end.**
- ☐ **I will speak up, especially when it is hard.**
- ☐ **I challenge my friends and family to be better.**
- ☐ **I practice allyship daily.**

- ☐ I commit to getting it right, while not being right.
- ☐ I challenge the status quo.
- ☐ I commit to doing things differently.
- ☐ I model the change I want to see.
- ☐ I recognize positive changes in others and myself.

JULIE KRATZ: SPEAKER / TRAINER / AUTHOR

Julie Kratz is a highly acclaimed TEDx speaker and inclusive leadership trainer who led teams and produced results in corporate America. After experiencing many career "pivot points" of her own, she started her own speaking business with the goal of helping leaders be more inclusive. Promoting diversity, inclusion, and allyship in the workplace, Julie helps organizations foster more inclusive environments. She is a frequent keynote speaker, podcast host, and executive coach. She holds an MBA from the Kelley School of Business at Indiana University, is a Certified Master Coach, and is a Certified Unconscious Bias Trainer, and Certified in Social Emotional Learning (SEL).

Her books include *Pivot Point: How to Build a Winning Career Game Plan*, *ONE: How Male Allies Support Women for Gender Equality*, and *Lead Like an Ally: A Journey Through Corporate America with Strategies to Facilitate Inclusion*, and her new children's book and coloring book, "The *Little Allies*."

Find Julie at NextPivotPoint.com, @NextPivotPoint, or on LinkedIn.

Works Cited

Shipman, Claire, Katty Kay, and JillEllyn Riley "Confidence Gap for Girls." *New York Times,* 2018.
https://www.nytimes.com/2018/10/01/well/family/confidence-gap-teen-girls-tips-parents.html

Albrecht, Karl. "The (Only) Five Fears We All Share." *Psychology Today*, 2012. https://www.psychologytoday.com/us/blog/brainsnacks/201203/the-only-5-fears-we-all-share

Bechdel Test Movie List. https://bechdeltest.com/

"Estimate of How Often LGBT Youth Attempt Suicide in the U.S." The Trevor Project, 2021. https://www.thetrevorproject.org/research-briefs/estimate-of-how-often-lgbtq-youth-attempt-suicide-in-the-u-s/

"Global Competencies." Participate Learning. https://www.participatelearning.com/global-competencies/

Harvard Implicit Bias Test. https://implicit.harvard.edu/Implicit/

McIntosh, Kristin, Emily Moss, and Jay Shambaugh. "Examining the Black and White Wealth Gap." Brookings, 2020. https://www.brookings.edu/blog/up-front/2020/02/27/examining-the-black-white-wealth-gap/

Menasce Horowitz, Juliana. "Americans See Advantages and Challenges in Growing Racial and Ethnic Diversity." Pew Research Center, 2019. https://www.pewresearch.org/social-trends/2019/05/08/americans-see-advantages-and-challenges-in-countrys-growing-racial-and-ethnic-diversity/

"More Than Meets the Eye." Royal Bromtom and Harefield Hospitals, 2021. https://www.rbht.nhs.uk/news/more-meets-eye-film-series-explores-non-visible-disabilities

Right Track Learning. Twitter post. March 23, 2021. https://twitter.com/RightTrack/status/1374324286828199937

"School Climate and Safety" U.S. Department of Education, Office for Civil Rights, 2018. https://www2.ed.gov/about/offices/list/ocr/docs/school-climate-and-safety.pdf

The Sentencing Project. "State Action to Narrow the School-to-Prison Pipeline", 2022. https://www.sentencingproject.org/

Smith, David G., W. Brad Johnson, and Lisen Stromberg. "How Men Can Be More Inclusive Leaders." *Harvard Business Review*, 2021. https://hbr.org/2021/05/how-men-can-be-more-inclusive-leaders

Walker, Tim. "Who Is the Average U.S. Teacher?" National Education Association, 2018. https://www.nea.org/advocating-for-change/new-from-nea/who-average-us-teacher

Winkler, Erin. "Children Are Not Colorblind." University of Wisconsin-Milwaukee, 2009. https://inclusions.org/wp-content/uploads/2017/11/Children-are-Not-Colorblind.pdf

Young, Natalie A. and Katrina Crankshaw. "U.S. Childhood Disability Rate up in 2019 from 2008." United States Census Bureau, 2021. https://www.census.gov/library/stories/2021/03/united-states-childhood-disability-rate-up-in-2019-from-2008.html

Made in United States
Orlando, FL
08 May 2022

17662989R00125